Border Design from a Traditional Zanzibari Kanga

Saud bin Ahmed Al Busaidi - Muscat, 2012

Memoirs of

An Omani Gentleman from Zanzibar

SAUD BIN AHMED AL BUSAIDI

WITH JANE JAFFER

Edited by

DR PATRICIA GROVES

The Historical Association of Oman

Memoirs of
an Omani Gentleman
from Zanzibar

Al Roya Press and Publishing House
P.O. Box 343, Postal Code 118, Al Harthy Complex, Muscat, Sultanate of Oman
Tel: (968) 24479888, Fax: (968) 24479889
E-mail: alroya@omantel.net.om   www.alroya.net

Publisher
Hatim Al Taie

Author
Saud bin Ahmed Al Busaidi

Design by
Dhian Chand, assisted by Dr Patricia Groves

Printed by
Modern Colour Printers
First Published February 2012

ISBN : 978-9948-16-248-3
Registration No: 18/2012

Hand carved catamaran on the shore of Blue Bay, Zanzibar

Contents

Dedication

This book is faithfully dedicated to my wonderful granddaughter, Roya Salim Al Lamki. It is my fondest wish that Roya and her generation shall inherit a world of greater peace and understanding.

Acknowledgements

First and foremost, I would like to express my gratitude to His Majesty Sultan Qaboos bin Said for all he has made possible for me and my fellow citizens. His Majesty led Oman's blessed Renaissance, creating a modern nation within the short span of four decades. Without His Majesty's remarkable wisdom, and his great concern for the people of this country, the Sultanate of Oman would not be the advanced and progressive nation that it is today.

I would like to formalize my personal appreciation of the thoughtfulness and vision of my granddaughter, Roya, for the key role she played in the creation of this book by encouraging me to write my memoirs and spearheading this project. I am tremendously grateful to writer, Mrs Jane Jaffer, the other key person on the project, for her hard work in assisting me in the creation of this book over the past two years. Without her tremendous commitment, the venture would not have come to fruition. Jane interviewed me at length, researched the historical background, recorded my stories, whether spoken or written, and assembled them into an initial chronicle.

I would also like to recognize author, Dr Patricia Groves, a colleague and friend of the family, for the fine work she accomplished in editing the book, enhancing and structuring the work to give it the excitement and flow I intended it to have. She also assisted ably with the production of the book.

My thanks go to my nephew, Barakat bin Ameen Al Busaidi, who showed great enthusiasm for the project. He contributed several old pictures that I had not seen before, which greatly enhance the book. From his research into our family history, Barakat was able to bring to life the story of our ancestors, some of whom were Governors of East Africa in domains that extended from Mogadishu to Malindi and along the Kenyan coast.

I am grateful to Mr Saud Al Mauly for his dedication, time and effort in helping me gain a broader perspective on various historical events that took place in Zanzibar. I also wish to thank Mr Issa Nasser Al Ismaily for his willingness to contribute relevant information in documenting some of the events described in my memoirs.

I am both pleased and honoured that the Historical Association of Oman has endorsed this book. Their support and encouragement is greatly valued.

The sponsors of this book, The Ramesh Khimji Group of Companies and Bank Muscat have been not only generous in contributing towards the publication costs, but also very enthusiastic about the project. Their altruism and support, along with their genuine interest in the content, has been inspiring to all of us. I would like to acknowledge Anne Bouji, Senior Manager, Book Publishing Al Roya Press and Publishing House who went beyond the call of duty in her work on the book. Al Roya was exceptionally helpful and genuinely shared our dedication to the project.

Last but not least, I would like to thank my lovely wife, Zakiya, for her patience and understanding during the many evenings when I worked on the book late into the night, recalling and recording my memoirs. Thank you for everything Zakiya.

I am tremendously grateful to these truly wonderful people – family and friends – for all they have done to help me make a book of my life that hopefully will be of value to a many readers within the Sultanate of Oman and Zanzibar, as well as on other shores in this increasingly small world.

Saud bin Ahmed Al Busaidi
Muscat, February 2012

From the Ramesh Khimji Group of Companies

It is well known that Zanzibar once shared the seat of power for a vast trading empire in the Indian Ocean Rim under the dominion of the famous Sayyid Said bin Sultan, Ruler of Oman and Zanzibar, but what is not so well known is what happened in the century-and-a-half following his reign.

This informative and fascinating book helps fill the gap by telling a continuous story against the background of life in Zanzibar, from the late nineteenth century when the author's grandfather arrived in Zanzibar, until the Revolution of 1964. The influence of the Zanzibar era in the history of Oman is still very much alive and social connections between the two countries contribute to the rich cosmopolitan fabric of the culture from which we all benefit.

The Ramesh Khimji Group of Companies also has its roots in the great seaborne trading era of the Sultanate. My ancestors came to Oman in 1870, at roughly the same time that Mr Saud bin Ahmed Al Busaidi's grandfather went to Zanzibar. This book speaks to all of us, evoking shared memories of the past and our joint ambitions for the future of the nation which we are working together to build. The Ramesh Khimji Group of Companies is proud to have played a role in bringing this book before readers in Oman and abroad who surely will feel blessed by the seasoned wisdom of the author, while enjoying his riveting story.

Ramesh Khimji, Chairman

www.rkhimjigroup.com

From Bank Muscat

Bank Muscat takes the greatest pleasure in supporting Omani heritage and culture. This book, which traces one man's journey through almost a century of the country's history, makes an important contribution to our understanding of the values of the nation and the courage of its people.

At the height of Oman's commercial power in the nineteenth century, Mr Saud bin Ahmed Al Busaidi's grandfather went off to seek his fortune in Zanzibar. He joined a community of hard-working, entrepreneurial Omanis who knew how to create wealth and helped develop Zanzibar into one of the strongest economies of the era. With a strong presence as the leading financial services provider in Oman, spurring economic expansion, Bank Muscat shares the values of Oman's original overseas pioneers.

On a personal note, I would like to say that I admire the ability and initiative of a man who in his ninety-sixth year undertook to write not simply his life story, but what really amounts to an historical drama. On behalf of Bank Muscat, it is a privilege to extend congratulations to this extraordinary gentleman on his truly remarkable achievement.

Abdulrazak Ali Issa, CEO

A note from Jane Jaffer

It has been a great privilege for me to document the memoirs of Saud bin Ahmed Al Busaidi. I have spent many enjoyable hours with the author discussing and recording his stories about the various people, places and events which have shaped his life. Despite his great age, Mr Al Busaidi's memory is both vivid and accurate and the picture he paints of his era is fascinating.

Saud bin Ahmed lived the first half of his life in East Africa where some of his ancestors had settled during the eighteenth and nineteenth centuries, becoming prominent figures in the political life of the region. After an idyllic childhood in Zanzibar, Mr Al Busaidi studied hard and entered the civil service. He was one of the first to receive a government scholarship which allowed him to study Public Administration at the University of Oxford. On his return to Zanzibar, Mr Al Busaidi rose through the ranks to become a District Commissioner. Closely connected to Zanzibar's royalty, and indeed brother-in-law to Sultan Khalifa bin Haroub Al Busaidi, the longest ruling Sultan of Zanzibar, the author experienced Zanzibar's golden era. He was a key figure in protocol, attending to heads of state and royalty. In his leisure time, Saud Al Busaidi pursued horse-back riding, polo, rowing, hunting and travel.

The author witnessed first hand the dark days of the Zanzibar Revolution and the story of his life following this shattering event is one that shows exceptional courage and adaptability. I believe this book has something to say not only to the people of East Africa and Oman, but to all people around the world, for its truths are universal.

Typical narrow street in Stone Town

Foreword

In the Sultanate of Oman, as in other parts of the Arab world, the family is at the very centre of our lives. Almost all social activities revolve around the family. Whether it is a birthday, a wedding or an Eid celebration, it is the family that is always at the heart of the occasion.

As we are growing up we admire and depend on our parents, but tend to know little of them as independent people or as separate personalities. It is hard to imagine them with an existence before they became our parents. We hear stories of their youth and have glimpses of our parents in their careers and outside concerns, but we really do not come to know them as fully as we do our siblings, close cousins and friends. There comes a time in life for most of us when we realize this and try to learn more about our parents – people who are so close to us and yet so strangely mysterious.

And so it was with great interest and fascination that I read my father's memoirs. I came to appreciate his overriding concern for the family, especially for my brother, my sister and me as children. Of course this is something that I knew, but to read a vivid account of this is to have another layer of happiness in the childhood memories that each one of us savours.

My father's lifetime, beginning almost a century ago now, encompasses momentous events in the history of Oman and Zanzibar. He was fortunate to be close to a panorama of interesting people in changing times; and to have the perceptive abilities to register something of the nature and historical import of the different eras he witnessed. His is a personal interpretation based on recollection over time, yet it rings with the truth of the times as professionally recorded by others.

My father was fortunate also to travel extensively and to have exciting adventures with wildlife and in his encounters with other cultures in times long past. Story-telling is deeply ingrained in the oral traditions of the Sultanate, and my father recounts his adventures with the charm of a true Omani storyteller – so much so, that at times I found myself reading his memoirs as if the stories were about a character in a novel - a familiar but new hero.

I am grateful to my father for the gift of his memoirs, as is the entire family, and I expect that succeeding generations will be as well. We are sharing this book with a larger readership because of its historical value, and in the hope that you will find it as interesting, educational and entertaining as we have.

Dr Rawya Saud Al Busaidi

Preface

It was my granddaughter Roya Salim Al Lamki who had the idea that I should write my memoirs. Roya has always been interested in the family history and loves to listen to my stories.

Roya envisioned a book as natural and lively as the story-telling which has long been a tradition in Omani culture. And so I thought the best approach was simply to tell the stories of my life to someone who could record all the details and put them together into the stream of my life.

The most formative experience in my life was undoubtedly the 1964 Revolution in Zanzibar - when I was fifty years old, married, with a family of three children, and settled in a good career. This violent revolution shattered the world as we knew it and left the lives of those who survived in ruins. But the human being is astonishingly resilient – and the second half of this book is about rebuilding a life – as almost all Omani Zanzibaris have done.

The book begins with the drama of the Revolution and then flashes back to 1914 when I was born on the peaceful shores of Zanzibar. The modern world had emerged and was about to demonstrate its new-found technological power in the First World War. In many ways, my story chronicles the changing times of the twentieth century, and I have endeavoured to place the personal within the larger historical context, but in an unobtrusive way, so that natural, unaffected story-telling remains the focal point.

At about the mid-point in the book, we reach the 1964 Zanzibar Revolution again – and the story then carries forward through several unsettled years until the ascension of His Majesty Sultan Qaboos bin Said to the throne of Oman in 1970. A momentous new era of change was ushered in, resulting in the creation of a true homeland for the thousands of Omanis who had fled the Revolution or were living abroad because of the difficult circumstances that prevailed before the advent of His Majesty Sultan Qaboos bin Said.

Those of us who loved Zanzibar did not lose it forever, and the book ends happily with holidays there in a family setting.

Chapter 1
The beginning of the end

Stone Town, 12th January, 1964 -

That night I decided to go to my club. On the way there I met an old man whom I knew was sympathetic to the rebellious Afro-Shirazi Party*. When I told him I was going to town, the old man reacted strangely. Nervous and on edge, he hesitated, his eyes darting this way and that. I think the old man was about to tell me something momentous, but changed his mind. With a shrug of his shoulders, the old man hurried on his way. Ironically, he wished me well.

These were troubled times. Normally, I would have been well aware of any rumblings, but, unexpectedly, just two weeks earlier, I had been transferred from my post in Stone Town to Mkokotoni where I was put in charge of the rural areas with my headquarters in an outpost twenty-four miles from town. As Urban District Commissioner of the area for a number of years, I had built up good relationships with many of the townspeople and always had my ear to the ground. In addition, I had a variety of intelligence sources to keep me informed of any underground movements or political agitation.

It was obvious that danger was in the air. I had argued against my sudden transfer from the capital, Zanzibar Town, as it seemed crucial in these circumstances for the government to remain well informed. The answers I was given did not make sense. I was beginning to suspect that the decision to transfer me had not been without design. My intuition was right. Later it became clear that some officials in the government had plotted with the revolutionaries. My transfer was part of an intrigue to keep the government in the dark.

* Prior to the 1964 Revolution, the leftist Afro-Shirazi Party (ASP) was formed by a union between the mostly Persian *Shirazi* Party and the mostly African *Afro* party.

1

The move was particularly unwelcome as I had felt a growing unease and tension in Stone Town. Staying well informed was essential if we were to be effective in preventing or stamping out any unrest during this period of growing instability.

When I arrived at the club that night, I found it unusually quiet, as though there were a self-imposed curfew. Trouble had been brewing for some time, and, sensing that danger might now be imminent, I asked the lone Indian police officer present what action had been taken to safeguard the town. The Officer assured me that all was well and that barriers had been erected on the roads at each point of entry from the hinterland to stop the rebels.

Although this was welcome news, somehow I felt uneasy, and immediately decided to go and inspect the five roads that connected the interior to the town in order to determine for myself how effective the barriers might be. What I discovered shocked me! There were no barriers whatsoever in place. Not a single one! How could this be?

On the way home, I was intensely preoccupied, worrying about what might happen. Things seemed to be falling apart. The anxiety I felt was tangible and not just in my body – it was all around - on the streets, in the buildings and in the very air I breathed. When I heard the ominous sound of gunfire in the distance, I knew that our world had changed irrevocably.

The rebel forces were advancing at an alarming speed. I could feel time running out like water through my fingers. I had no doubt that the armed mob marching aggressively into town from all sides would leave a horrific trail of death and destruction in their wake. With mounting anxiety, I rushed home, slamming and bolting the door. I did not even think of sleep. Instead, I paced the floor ceaselessly.

At one o'clock in the morning, I was jolted by the telephone ringing. It was a request to go straight to Police Headquarters to strategize with the Chief of Police and make arrangements for the town's defence. I knew I was risking my life by leaving the house, but I also understood that failure to act decisively with the looming threat of an armed conflict would be disastrous.

It was already too late. Once outside, I could hear the unmistakable sound of gun battles raging all over the area. I made it to Police Headquarters and stayed there until 3:00 a.m. when about a dozen desperate policemen came running over from their headquarters saying that they could no longer hold out as they had run out of ammunition. These men had repeatedly called the Commissioner of Police asking him to come with the key to the Police Headquarters' armoury. The Commissioner said he would come, but did not.

It seemed very strange to me that the police had not been issued with a key to the ammunition depot and that the Commissioner was stonewalling his own men. Why? Things were looking increasingly ominous. Without access to ammunition, what hope did the police have of stemming the tide and stopping the onslaught of masses of well-armed Rebels? The European Advisor to the Prime Minister was called and informed of the situation. He told us that the British Commander had gone to Malindi Station in Stone Town and urged us to go there as soon as possible.

I rushed off to Malindi where I found the British Commander deep in conversation with his local assistant. I had no sooner walked into the room than I offered to help in any way I could. Imagine my shock and surprise when I was told that my help was not needed! With rising frustration boiling over into anger, I went back to my office where, around 5:00 a.m., I received a call with orders to report to the airport to receive a British contingent from Kenya that apparently had been sent to negotiate a peace settlement. I would later discover that the Kenyan authorities had not allowed the plane to leave for Zanzibar.

At this point I understood why the key to the Police armoury had not been issued – it was so that the weapons could not be used to defend the town. I also realized that the strategy behind my transfer was to replace me with a commissioner who would ensure that the government would not be informed of the rebel advance.

I knew that driving to the airport would be extremely dangerous and took the precaution of checking on the situation before I left. I noticed with considerable unease that my hand was shaking as I dialled the number for the airport. The phone rang for some time before my good friend, Mr Ali Khalifa Al Miskiry, who was in charge of the airport, picked up the receiver. The moment Ali spoke, I could hear the panic in his voice. He said the fighting had intensified and it was clear that no planes would be arriving that day. As the rapidly advancing rebels were already nearing the airport, my friend advised me not to come, saying that even he was about to leave. The situation was indeed grim.

After a few minutes, the Advisor to the Prime Minister phoned to say I should not go to the airport as the British contingent from Kenya was not coming. In the meantime, a rebel contingent was advancing toward the police station. They made two attempts to take the station, but were repulsed. From the window of my office I witnessed the assaults during which several rebels were shot dead and lay motionless in the blood-stained dust. The horror of war was right there in front of my eyes and the worst was yet to come.

The Oath of Loyalty which governed our behaviour as senior government officials in extreme circumstances would not allow us to leave our stations without orders. Thankfully, a call soon came and

4

we were advised to go home. I had not been home long when an alarming announcement came over the radio. It was President Karume demanding that all Civil Servants report immediately to their respective government offices to hand over their keys. Obviously the Rebels were now in full control.

On the first day of the Revolution, Mr Abeid Amani Karume (1905 -1972) was declared President of Zanzibar. On the second day, he paid a visit to all central government departments to appropriate the keys to every office, including mine, that of the District Commissioner. The situation was clearly worsening. We were all extremely apprehensive, like hanging on the edge of a cliff, not knowing how long we could hold out and what might happen next.

On the third day, a young man, a follower of Babu, the so-called communist leader, walked unannounced into my office and rudely spoke to me in a voice that cracked with forced authority. *"Come with me to the police station,"* he said as threateningly as he could. In spite of his youth and inexperience - or perhaps because of it - I was shocked and alarmed, especially knowing that I could do nothing except comply with his order. A cold chill went down my spine.

The police station was right next to my office building. With increasing trepidation, I followed the young man to the station where he handed me over, as if I were a criminal, to the police officer in charge. I found myself watching as my young captor disappeared through a back door like an evil spirit. After a while, a truck arrived loaded with nervous government officials and employees, all of whom had been unceremoniously arrested. With them, I was hauled away to the *Voice of Zanzibar* Radio Station.

We were led upstairs to a large room where we found the revolutionary leaders sitting together, backs straight, chests puffed out with the raw thrill of freshly gained power. With strange solemnity, they ordered us to raise our hands in the air as if we were enemies who had just surrendered to their superior might. It was an extremely tense and oddly surreal moment. I no longer felt like myself, but like a stranger in alien circumstances. We did not know what our captors would do next. In my inner mind, I feared we were going to be shot.

Then I heard authoritative boot steps drawing nearer. A man from Kenya by the name of Okello who had just been made a General was coming to inspect us. This was apparently the man who had led the rebellion. Okello walked up and down the line, each footstep falling on the floor with a hard thud. The General's face was darkly cast in a harsh demeanour. Abruptly calling on the guards, Okello ordered us all to be taken away. With hearts sinking in the quicksand of our shaken bodies, we were captives going we knew not where. The fear I felt was ice cold. At that moment, I had little hope of a positive outcome for me or for my beloved Zanzibar.

Marshall John Okello (centre front) and the Revolutionaries

Chapter 2
How it all began

Omani communities had been established in Zanzibar and other parts of East Africa long before the dramatic events of the Revolution of 1964. The links between Oman and East Africa in centuries past were the result of trade powered by an invisible force – the monsoon winds that sailing ships from Oman rode swiftly southward in the autumn, and northward in the spring. Trading connections eventually led to marriage and settlement. With its exceptionally rich soil and abundant economic opportunities, Zanzibar in particular had enormous appeal for people from desert lands.

The Ruler of Oman, Sayyid Said bin Sultan (1804-1856), known as 'The Great', was a man of vision who extended his trading domain from the waters of the Arabian Gulf to the western Indian Ocean Rim and along the eastern coast of Africa. In the early 1840's when the tremendous potential of Zanzibar for wealth creation became apparent, Sayyid Said made a shrewd decision - to establish a second capital for his trading empire - in Zanzibar Town, the main city on the Island. With Sayyid Said's rise to power in the East African domain, Omanis were encouraged to immigrate to the lands under his control and contribute to their development.

Among those who heard the call of a fabled island in faraway seas was a prominent member of the ruling Al Busaidi clan - my grandfather, Sayyid Hammad bin Ahmed Al Busaidi, who lived on the northern coast of Oman in the isolated fishing village of Barka where he was born and brought up. Distinguished by a landmark fort guarding the coast and monitoring the hinterland, the old settlement was sustained by agriculture as well as fishing.

Nevertheless, life in nineteenth-century Barka was far from easy as resources were limited and the climate was harsh, especially in the gruelling summer months from March to October when temperatures soared to well above 40 degrees Celsius. The only respite was to shelter in airy palm-frond houses built in the cooling shade of date-palm orchards for use in summer.

It was in the 1880's when my grandfather took the momentous decision to leave the only home he had ever known and follow his dream of a much better life in Zanzibar. Gathering his courage and a few belongings, my grandfather said goodbye to my grandmother, Sayyida Khoula, and their two young children as unemotionally as he could, then quickly mounted his camel and rode off through the dust of the desert. He had no idea when he would see his family again.

Day after day, from dawn to dusk, Sayyid Hammad traveled along rough tracks in the sand, just as his ancestors, the Al bu Saids, had long

Omani notables in Barka - 1914

ago, when, in search of a more promising land, they travelled through the unforgiving deserts of Yemen and southern Oman. Eventually they reached the oasis of Adam in the central interior of Oman where they established a settlement that flourished. Facing a much longer journey across oceans as well as desert, but with equal valour, my grandfather hoped for as fortuitous an outcome.

Sayyid Hammad's first destination was the port of Mutrah, once the commercial hub of what is now the capital region of Oman. There my grandfather sold his weary camel to the highest bidder and made his way to the harbour front where he purchased a ticket for the next dhow to Bombay which would arrive when the winds were favourable.

Several days later when the ship came into harbour, a large crowd gathered to meet relatives and watch the unloading of cargo. I can almost hear the wooden boards of the old dhow creaking as the passengers boarded. And in my mind's eye I see the diminutive ship leaving the harbour, with my grandfather standing on deck watching the majestic Hajar Mountains, and his beloved country, slowly disappear from view. Then, embracing an unknown future, he abruptly turned his face to the open sea.

Sayyid Hammad made friends among his fellow passengers, enjoying the close camaraderie that develops on an extended ocean voyage. Together they endured the extreme conditions of the journey on rolling waves in cramped quarters, as there were no cabins or basic amenities on the old dhow, let alone any conveniences. Many days of monotony compounded by dampness and discomfort were to go by before the ship docked and unloaded in the chaotic bustle of Bombay.

9

Then as now, the port of the old city was teeming with life and colour, with all kinds of boats coming and going, a maze of narrow lanes, small shops, fast-moving rickshaws, slow ox carts, thronging pedestrians and rickety bicycles. Alone in this crowded city, struggling to get his land legs back, and wearing his distinctive Omani gown and turban, Sayyid Hammad was immediately spotted as a new arrival and besieged by beggars as he made his way through jam-packed streets to secure his lodgings.

Venturing out to find a congenial place to eat, my grandfather, weary but excited, pondered the next segment of his journey over a meal of fresh baked bread and hot curry. Already far from home, his ultimate destination still lay thousands of miles away in unknown territory which he hoped against hope would be a promised land.

It was thankfully not a dhow but a large and reasonably comfortable steamship that took my grandfather from Bombay out into the open Indian Ocean and down the coast of East Africa. Along with passengers, the vessel carried a rich cargo of trading goods – cotton, tea, rice, coffee, and spices including turmeric, cumin, coriander and nutmeg.

Lasting more than three weeks, the voyage was through frequently rough seas that battered the ship and soaked anyone on deck, but there were many days when the water was calm and glittering with bright sunshine. In these interludes, the passengers would watch sea birds and sometimes sight dolphins and whales.

After days and days of viewing nothing but endless ocean, it must have been incredibly exciting when first Pemba, and then Zanzibar appeared like shimmering mirages on the horizon. As the ship drew closer, the rich red soil and lush green vegetation of Zanzibar came into

Present day Zanzibar Town from the sea

sight – a far cry from the deserts of Arabia. The best was yet to come with temperate weather, easy-going people, and a thrilling sense of abundance, signalled by the pungent smell of cloves which fuelled the Island's wealth.

It was not long after first light when the ship entered the outer waters of Zanzibar. In that moment it seemed that the whole Island shone in the rosy glow of a freshly risen sun. Slender dugout canoes and light catamarans with white sails zoomed over the shimmering waters toward the ship amid shouts of welcome in Swahili. With a gladdened heart, my grandfather hastened down one of the ship's old wooden ladders and slipped into a small boat heading for the emerald and turquoise waters of the inner harbour.

Bait Al Ajaib, The House of Wonders

The old Arab Fort in Stone Town

Dr. Patricia Groves

On shore, amid coconut palms, were the minarets of Zanzibar Town, its wide sweep of whitewashed buildings, the towers and battlements a seventeenth-century fort and the verandas and lavish rococo doors of a beautiful palace known as 'The House of Wonders' (Bait Al Ajaib).

Built in 1883 as a ceremonial Palace for Sultan Barghash, Bait Al Ajaib was known as The House of Wonders because it was the first house in Zanzibar to have electricity and an elevator. Bait Al Ajaib had enormous doors, resplendent in elaborate carving and gilt decoration. Brass lions guarded the entrance.

As Sayyid Hammad at last stood on solid ground in his dream destination, his profound sense of satisfaction in a mission accomplished was shot through with apprehension. Where would he go now? How would he find his fortune? His gaze encompassed Bait Al Sahel, the stately white palace with a grand gallery of coloured glass and graceful arched verandahs overlooking the harbour. An ornately carved wooden door marked the entrance to the royal residence. Little did Sayyid Hammad know then that he would walk many times through those doors in a life intimately linked with the inhabitants of the palace.

The narrow streets of the inner town near the harbour might have reminded my grandfather of Mutrah, were it not for the exotic goods, the slow rhythm of activity and the distinctly African ambience. Leaving the noise and clamour behind, he wandered into the smartest area of nineteenth-century Zanzibar Town where the streets were cooled by fountains. Tall white townhouses with handsome balconies and latticed windows graced the neighbourhood. My grandfather came upon a beautiful white mosque; and, in answer to the call to prayer, he profoundly thanked Allah for bringing him safely to the wondrous shores of Zanzibar.

13

View from the Palace Museum in Stone Town

Stone Town as seen from the courtyard of the old fort

Chapter 3
My grandfather's early adventures in Zanzibar

In the lush tropical climate of Zanzibar, the coconut palms that originally grew in the wild flourished on numerous plantations where coconuts were harvested as food and also refined to produce copra, oil, and soap. Apart from extracting the juice, making copra was the simplest manufacturing process, as it was purely a matter of drying quantities of coconut flesh or 'meat' in the plentiful sunshine of the island. A staple commodity in the local economy, dried copra was bundled for transport to the harbour where it was loaded on ships for export to buyers, mostly in France.

When my grandfather first saw donkey carts piled high with copra streaming into town, something clicked - an idea flashed. He could buy the coconut harvest from a local plantation owner, make copra, and sell it for quick cash. His funds were limited but he could manage to make the initial investment, and so it was not long before my grandfather was a player in the brisk copra trade.

As an active businessman, Sayyid Hammad came across many prominent people in Zanzibar. Sayyid Khalid bin Barghash, a cousin of the Ruler, Sultan Hamed bin Thuwaini, became a close friend of my grandfather and confided in him. The two friends spent many hours together talking politics and discussing their hopes for the future of Zanzibar. My grandfather soon understood that, in keeping with his royal blood, Sayyid Khalid had rather high ambitions.

The opportunity to act on ambition came in 1896 when Sultan Hamed bin Thuwaini died without issue and the throne was momentarily vacant.

In a lightening-fast reaction, Sayyid Khalid and his supporters, including my grandfather, stealthily made their way to the palace in the dead of night. Crawling through a window, they easily gained access to the state offices where everything was at their disposal. Men with a mission, they worked with determined efficiency right throughout the night, making whatever arrangements they could to usurp power. The following morning Sayyid Khalid bin Barghash officially declared himself the new Sultan of Zanzibar.

As might be expected, the British were not amused. They had in mind someone favourable to their interests - Sayyid Hamoud bin Mohammed. Since Zanzibar was a protectorate under their aegis, the British had the power to get what they wanted. Straight away, they sent word to Sayyid Khalid, ordering him to lower his flag by nine o'clock on the 27th of August 1896 and immediately vacate the Palace.

When Sayyid Khalid and his supporters failed to comply with this request, the 'Shortest War in History' ensued.* British warships opened fire on Stone Town, destroying the palace, the harem, the Sultan's ship and the lighthouse. Bait Ajaib, the House of Wonders, was also damaged, but not heavily.

* On August 25, 1896, Sayyid Khalid bin Barghash seized power and assembled an army of 2,800 men. On August 26, Sayyid Khalid and his men fortified the Palace and anchored the Sultan's armed yacht, the *Glasgow,* in the harbor in front of the Palace. To counter these moves, the British assembled five cruisers in the harbour. They then landed several parties of Royal Marines on the shore. At 8:00 am on August 27, an ultimatum was issued to Sayyid Khalid that he vacate the Palace within one hour or hostilities would commence. At 9:02 the British ships opened fire. After sinking the *Glasgow*, they pounded the palace, forcing Sayyid Khalid to raise the white flag. The war lasted approximately 45 minutes.

16

Although no lives were lost, serious injuries were sustained. My grandfather mentioned that the walls of the royal palace were adorned with many beautiful gold-gilded mirrors. As the British fired from their warships, the mirrors shattered from the vibrations of the cannon blasts, and lethal shards of glass flew through the air, injuring many among the hundreds of courtiers, royals and staff who inhabited the palace. Chaos ensued as hundreds of people, including women and children, fled for their lives, scattering in all directions.

During the bombardment, Sayyid Khalid and my grandfather were on the verandah of the Palace, where fortunately they were not in the line of fire. As hostilities began, they knew they did not stand a chance of holding their ground, and so, quickly disguising themselves, they escaped through a side entrance. It is said that Sayyid Khalid sought asylum in the German Consulate and was sheltered there. A mere forty-five minutes after it had commenced, the Anglo-Zanzibar War was over, and the British declared Sayyid Hamoud bin Mohammed the new Sultan of Zanzibar.

Much later, I met the man who, during the violent bombardment of this rather inglorious war was ordered by Sayyid Khalid to climb up the stairs onto the roof of the besieged palace and raise the white flag of surrender. Of course there was no white flag to be found on the roof, so this innovative man took off his undergarment and hastily tied it to a stick. He was astonished when seconds after he waved his humble white garment, the firing ceased. Nevertheless, the Palace was virtually destroyed, with only the walls on the north side remaining. The new regime immediately undertook the reconstruction, and, four decades later, in 1936, the Royal Palace was completely renovated and modernised.

My grandfather said that, in the aftermath of the coup, he found the situation in Zanzibar disconcerting. As a relative newcomer to Zanzibar, he could not fathom the politics of the British rule. Life under a regime with a monarch who was obviously indebted to the British and acted accordingly, was at odds with my grandfather's vision of life in Zanzibar. He had come to Zanzibar confident that the nation would be governed in the familiar Omani way by a fellow countryman with predictable royal habits. When he realised this was, in effect, not the case, Sayyid Hammad decided to return to Oman.

But that was not the end of the story...

Chapter 4
Zanzibar becomes home

Overjoyed to see his family again and settling back into a relatively quiet life in Barka with all the old familiar things, my grandfather experienced a measure of contentment that soon began to wane. He found himself eagerly awaiting news from Zanzibar that came by dhow only once a year when Omani traders returned to Muscat with the seasonal monsoon winds. Sayyid Hammad could not deny that he was still immensely interested in Zanzibar. When, in a few year's time, he got word that the Island was stable again, that business was thriving, and there appeared to be less interference from the British, my grandfather decided to return.

Arriving back on the verdant shores of Zanzibar in high spirits, my grandfather was eager to resume his former life with old and new friends. He felt fortunate to find the Island as stable and prosperous as anticipated - and took up his copra business with renewed energy. But nothing is ever perfect; and however thrilling it was at first, my grandfather began to find his work in supervising the copra production stressful, as he did not speak or understand Swahili well enough for ease of communication with his African employees.

It must have been at this stage that my grandfather paused to reflect on life. Counting his many blessings, he decided that the time had come to express his gratitude for all he had been given and make the great pilgrimage, or Hajj, to the holy city of Mecca, as every Muslim who has the means must do at least once during his or her lifetime.

Sayyid Hammad embarked on the pilgrimage with his close friend, Sheikh Nasser Al Ismaily. When the pair arrived at Jeddah, they were strongly urged to hire guards for protection on the road to

Mecca. They were warned that if they travelled unaccompanied, they would be confronted by tribesmen demanding payment of 'taxes' for the right to cross their lands. Daring and foolhardy, the two friends decided not to wait to be assigned guards. Instead, they straight away bought camels and packed their saddle bags with the necessary provisions. Taking the precaution of arming themselves with loaded muskets in case of what they deemed the unlikely eventuality of an attack – they were ready to go.

And so a lone caravan of two set forth on the long road to Mecca. Having journeyed all day long without incident, they were feeling quite confident and self-satisfied. But, just as night began to fall, they were unnerved by the sound of galloping camels. The next moment they saw, through a great cloud of dust, a band of fierce tribesmen thundering towards them. As they raced ahead at break-neck speed, Hammad and Nasser fired their muskets at the fast-pursuing bandits. Several rounds of bullets were exchanged as the camels galloped faster and faster. In grave danger, the two pilgrims whipped their camels to pick up speed in a chase that would last far into the night.

Somehow my grandfather and the Sheikh, outraced their attackers, escaping with their lives. The bandits finally gave up, but the two harried pilgrims did not stop until they arrived in Mecca – unharmed, but badly shaken. The same was not true of the camels which were calm, as camels always are, and seemed to know that much of the credit was theirs.

The hajj was the deeply moving experience that my grandfather had hoped it would be and he went back to his ordinary existence in Zanzibar fortified with inspiration and a strong sense of optimism. It was at this point that his life became increasingly intertwined with that of the Royal Family. Sometime prior to 1911, my grandfather became friends with Sayyid Khalifa bin Haroub, a man whom he had first met in

Oman many years earlier. My grandfather's friend, Sayyid Khalifa, was destined to succeed his brother-in-law, Sultan Ali bin Hamoud, who ruled from 1902 to 1911. Sayyid Khalifa would have the longest reign of any ruler of Zanzibar. It would last more than half a century - from December 1911 to October 1960.

Sultan Ali bin Hamoud was brought up in England and educated at Harrow. When he ascended the throne, Sayyid Ali's first project was to start a school worthy of his royal name – the Sultan's School. At that time, the people of Zanzibar had begun to realize the importance of good schooling and learning English; and so they were most appreciative of the Monarch's initiative. The new emphasis on education and qualifications encouraged several well-off families to send their children abroad for studies, in particular, to Egypt and to England. This progressive ruler was also credited with having brought the first car, a Daimler, to Zanzibar.

HH Ali bin Hamoud Al Busaidi, Sultan of Zanzibar, 1902-1911

Enlightened and action-oriented, Sultan Ali soon found that he was not comfortable with the circumstances of Zanzibar at that time. He did not take to life in Zanzibar and was not on good terms with the British Consul. The Monarch felt that the consul played a meddling rather than a supportive role. He resented the fact that this unwanted British official seemed to interfere in almost everything he tried to do. The seriously displeased Sultan took the trouble of sending formal letters of complaint to the British Government, but to no avail. Discouraged, Sultan Ali began to spend most of his time in England and France.

In the Sultan's absence, the country was ruled by British officials. Naturally, this did not please his subjects, particularly the old Arab dignitaries. In the conduct of their businesses, local residents found it awkward, and indeed, sometimes extremely annoying, to have to go to Major Francis Pearce, who held the post of British Resident from 1911 to 1922, or to other British officials. And this was especially true of Omani residents. One of those who objected to the excessive control of the British was my maternal grandmother, Sayyida Aisha Said Al Busaidi. My grandmother told me that she had once become so angry with the obstructions of Major Pearce that she threw her documents on his desk and stormed out of his office.

It was, to say the least, not at all convenient to have a monarch who, as much as possible, avoided living in his country. This had a negative impact on morale throughout the Island - with pervasive consequences. One of the outcomes was that people began to attribute the Sultan's unfavourable attitude toward his own country to the fact that he was educated abroad from an early age. This had the effect of discouraging many parents from sending their children overseas to study. An insular attitude developed that no doubt was a factor in slowing down the educational development of the people of Zanzibar.

For many decades, only primary education was available to the children of Zanzibar. When they finished school, young people could not find work in government offices since their qualifications were not up to the standard set by British officials. As the British preferred to appoint ready-made officials with a good knowledge of English, they imported civil servants from India. This made young Zanzibaris very bitter.

The situation later improved when the British decided to expand access to education by building schools deep into the countryside. The matter of qualified teachers became a pressing issue, and, eventually, a Teacher Training Institute was established. A higher standard of education was the result and graduates were considered qualified for positions in Government.

In June 1911, accompanied by Sayyid Khalifa bin Haroub, Sultan Ali bin Hamoud attended King George V's coronation in London. Ironically, this would turn out to be one of Sultan Ali's last official duties, as several months later, he decided to abdicate, abandoning Zanzibar forever. In consultation with the leaders of the Arab community, the British chose Sayyid Khalifa bin Haroub bin Thuwaini as the new Sultan of Zanzibar.

So it was that my grandfather's good friend, Sayyid Khalifa bin Haroub, who was born in Oman and had come to Zanzibar as a young man, became the tenth ruler of Zanzibar in the Al Busaidi Dynasty that began with Sayyid Said. The coronation took place on the 9th of December 1911 at Bait al Ajaib, the famed 'House of Wonders'.

Sultan Khalifa was a popular monarch who ruled Zanzibar until he died on the 9th of October 1960 - almost five decades after his coronation. The year before his investiture he married Sayyida Matuka, daughter of the eighth Ruler, Hamoud bin Mohammed, and

*HH Sayyid Khalifa bin Haroub Al Busaidi ruled Zanzibar from 1911-1960 **

* As Sayyid Khalifa was well loved by his people, there was great rejoicing on his Silver Jubilee in 1936. Grand celebrations took place, including an elaborate procession in the streets and the ceremonial opening of the Forodhani Gardens to the strains of the Sultan's military band. His Highness planted a tree that is still standing today.

sister of the ninth, his predecessor, Sayyid Ali bin Hamoud. Almost three decades later, in the late 1930's, Sayyid Khalifa would marry my dear sister, Sayyida Nunuu.

My sister, Sayyida Nunuu, wife of the Sultan of Zanzibar - 1958

My grandfather was honoured with the elevated post of Chief Courtier to HH Sultan Khalifa, soon becoming his right hand man. But all the while, he sorely missed his family and was even contemplating a return to Oman. Sayyid Khalifa suggested an attractive alternative - that Sayyid Hammad bring his family to Zanzibar as a benefit of his post. My grandfather accepted with gratitude, quickly dispatching a letter to his wife faraway in Barka, asking her to make arrangements to bring the family to Zanzibar.

When she received the letter, my grandmother, Sayyida Khoula Badr bin Hamid Al Busaidi, was jubilant as she had naturally found it difficult to manage with her husband so far away for such a long time. She once confided in me that she was very lonely and sometimes broke down in tears. And so, it was with a full heart that Sayyida Khoula packed her belongings and those of her two young children, Ahmed and Farshu. As it was not customary for a woman to travel alone, Sayyida Khoula and the children were accompanied by a revered older relative, Shaib bin Nasser Al Busaidi. With mixed feelings of joy and trepidation, Sayyida Khoula and her small party set out on the long voyage over unknown seas to a new life that was hard for her to imagine.

The first stop was Muscat where they stayed in the home of Sayyid Ahmed bin Mohammed Al Busaidi. In a few days, they would board a ship to Bombay just as my grandfather had, and then journey onward to the coast of East Africa to Zanzibar. Many years later when I came to visit him, Sayyid Ahmed told me about my family's stay at his house in Muscat. He said that the small boy, Ahmed, my father, enjoyed playing war games, and that he and his sister, Farshu, would spend the entire day running around chasing each other. Sayyid Ahmed left an indelible impression on me, as he was the only person I knew who had met my father when he was a small boy.

The journey from Oman via Bombay to Zanzibar was quite an adventure for Sayyid Hammad's young family, as never before had they left their homeland. My grandmother later related a sad story about the voyage from Bombay to Zanzibar. On board was a very beautiful Indian lady adorned with a great quantity of heavy gold jewellery who kept to herself and had an air of mystery about her. Obviously extremely wealthy, the enigmatic lady was often seen walking on deck in the evening, under the stars. However, one morning the beautiful lady with the golden jewellery failed to appear.

The crew checked the lady's cabin, but there was no sign of her. The lady had gone missing. A thorough search of the vessel ensued, but the beautiful Indian lady with all the gold was never seen again. Everyone felt a sense of unease. My grandmother and the other passengers could only assume that the unfortunate woman had been robbed of her magnificent jewellery by thieves and then thrown overboard.

One morning weeks later, my grandfather was sitting pleasantly with Sultan Khalifa in the sunshine on the verandah of the Palace overlooking the harbour when the Sultan drew my grandfather's attention to a British India ship that had just anchored in the still blue waters beyond the verandah. Could it be possible that his family was on the British India ship out there in the harbour? Sayyid Hammad laughed, saying that he had received no word at all from his family, so he doubted very much if they had even left Barka.

Sayyid Khalifa ordered his tripod and binoculars to be brought to the verandah. Sure enough, through the lens the Sultan saw an Omani woman with excited young children who were running about on the deck. He then quietly handed the binoculars to my grandfather. Skeptically, Sayyid Hammad surveyed the ship deck. Much to his astonishment, he spotted Khoula, Ahmed and Farshu! Letting out a cry of joy, he leapt out of his chair and ran down to the harbour where he got into the nearest boat and headed for the ship. What a wonderful reunion it was, with children jumping up and down and warm embraces all around. Sayyid Hammad knew that at last he would be happily settled in Zanzibar.

During this time of peace and prosperity, my grandfather's life was full. He moved into a large house with his family where all the pleasures of a settled domestic existence were his again. Sayyid Hammad worked diligently on state affairs, but also enjoyed a busy social life at the Royal Court as well as in leisure activities arranged by the Sultan. Sayyid

Khalifa was an enthusiastic sportsman who loved sailing, horseback riding, and playing polo. He was a monarch who knew the value of relaxation; and he would go sailing any afternoon that he was not engaged in official functions.

All the while, there were children to attend to. My grandfather arranged for his son, my father, Sayyid Ahmed bin Hammad, to go to a good school in Zanzibar. One of the teachers was an Egyptian named Mohammed bin Abdul Bari whom my grandfather knew personally. He was thus able to ensure that the teacher paid particular attention to the schooling of his son, including handwriting skills, considered extremely important in that era. My father was a serious student who needed little encouragement to study hard and apply what he had learned. Over the years in school and under the guidance of my grandfather, my father became an accomplished young man capable of working in government without further training.

When the First World War broke out in 1914, Zanzibar declared war on Germany. It was a momentous time in world history and Zanzibar was involved in the action. In September 1914, *HMS Pegasus,* a British warship, was sunk in Zanzibar Harbour by the German cruiser, *Koningsberg.* Apparently fishermen in the area who were actually German spies had informed the Captain of the German warship that a British ship was in harbour – or at least that's what people said.

It was also during the War that an airplane first landed in Zanzibar. Not long after this milestone in the modern history of Zanzibar, Sultan Khalifa became the first ruler of Zanzibar to have the privilege of viewing his kingdom from the air. All the while, times were rapidly changing. The world had never seen a war on this scale or with such powerful technology capable of mass destruction. This was the era into which I was born.

Chapter 5
My entry into the world

In accordance with the long-held Omani custom, as soon as my father, Sayyid Ahmed, came of age, his parents arranged a suitable match for him. The bride-to-be was Sayyida Kalthoum Suleiman Al Busaidi, daughter of Kenyan-born Hamed bin Suleiman Al Busaidi, a civil contractor who worked in construction on the coast of Kenya and later settled in Zanzibar.

My father must have been delighted with his parents' choice, for by all accounts my mother was a beautiful woman - tall, and slim, with big brown eyes and long black hair. I remember how much I admired my mother, and how lovely she was. I knew her to be a very lively and engaging person - full of fun, with a ready smile and alert, sparkling eyes; yet, paradoxically, she could be quite shy in company outside the family.

On the 15th of September in 1914 at the family house in Malindi, Zanzibar, Sayyida Kalthoum gave birth to me, her third and last child. Unfortunately, my older brother had died when he was a child, and so my older sister, Sayyida Nunuu, was to be my only sibling. She became a lifelong friend.

My maternal grandmother, Aisha Said Al Busaidi, told me that the details of my birth were simply written on a piece of paper, since, in the old days in Zanzibar, there was no official registration of births. That humble piece of paper was kept in the family's heirloom copy of the Holy Qu'ran, from which it eventually vanished. Nevertheless, my grandmother was quite certain of the date of my birth.

29

As was the custom in families such as ours, I had a nurse who became a central figure in my upbringing. She was a wonderful Zanzibari woman named Ambra whose mother had been in our service . Ambra lived with our family for her entire life and tended to my every need as I was growing up. From my earliest years, I have fond memories of Ambra telling me stories every night before going to bed and softly singing sweet lullabies such as: *Kitundu, Princess flying in a basket, take me to my mother...*

Sometimes to entertain me, Ambra would jump up and dance like a *shaitan* (devil). Naturally I loved this and would laugh and clap my hands as my normally sedate nurse twirled around the room. Once I asked Ambra whether she was invited to *shaitan* dances and if she would take me next time. Alas, the answer was one that children hear so often – *"Children are not allowed".*

I also had a very close bond with my grandmother, Sayyida Aisha. This strong connection, my grandmother explained, began with me crying a lot at night as a baby. My parents' house was separated from my grandmother's by only a narrow lane. When she heard me crying, my grandmother would call through the window to my father, asking him to bring the baby to her. Grandmother Aisha knew that I cried because I was hungry, but she did not share this secret with my parents, as she wanted her new grandchild to be with her as much as possible. As soon as my father was gone, my grandmother would prepare a light porridge and feed me. Almost immediately I would stop crying and my parents never understood why. For them it remained a mystery.

My grandmother Aisha loved and cherished me throughout her life. During her final days when she was confined to bed, she asked my mother to call me to her bedside. When I came, my grandmother requested me to change her orientation in bed. My mother remarked that she would have been glad to do this for my grandmother. Well, of course, my grandmother just wanted me to be close to her; and she firmly replied, *"My grandson knows better how to turn me around."*

Grandmother Aisha was a wonderful person who always thought of others. When her time had come, my grandmother asked all her relatives and close friends to come to see her so that she could say a last goodbye to each and every one of them personally. More than thirty ladies arrived, and my grandmother began the poignant goodbyes. With her dying breath, she told the ladies to stay close together and to love and help each other.

I think it was Plato who said that a person's character is shaped by the age of five. This may well be true. My earliest experiences were of an environment brimming with love and care, in the family home with my parents and sister, in the extended family, as well as in our larger social circle. I believe that this sustained me through the many trials we face in life and that it also made times of happiness and joy more precious and deeply felt.

The Author wearing the Al Said turban in Zanzibar in 1945

Chapter 6
Growing up in remarkable times

In the years following the First World War (1914-1918), an influenza pandemic swept around the globe and many people in Zanzibar were affected. Sadly, my father, Ahmed, was one of them. He died when I was just three years old. It was a devastating loss for our family.

Despite the tragedy of losing my father at such a young age, I have many happy memories of my childhood and youth. As I was growing up in the Malindi neighbourhood where Sayyid Khalid bin Mohammed bin Said bin Sultan, elder brother of Sultan Hamoud bin Mohammed and uncle of HH Sultan Ali bin Hamoud lived, we made frequent visits to his house. I have vivid memories of these visits which never failed to be interesting as well as eventful. Sayyid Khalid was a very impressive man - six feet tall with a noble face, a fine beard and a full head of thick silvery hair. A commanding personage, Sayyid Khalid had a voice so deep and penetrating that the room positively vibrated when he spoke.

Sayyid Khalid had two distinguished sisters, Sayyida Alya and Sayyida Fatma, who were important, well-loved figures in my childhood. Unusual for the times and for women of their status, the two royal ladies never married. In spite of being 'spinsters', Sayyida Alya and Sayyida Fatma were revered by the people and not just because they were royal - they were generous, caring, and highly religious.

We had such happy times in my childhood years that I would not have traded my life for anyone else's. Since we did not have many toys, we would create things to play with. My favourite was a primitive car fashioned from planks of wood. I would sit in that funny wooden car and use my feet to make it move along. I also amused myself by spinning a wheel with a stick, daydreaming as it spun and spun. Sometimes we would play dominoes or a game of counting shells called 'Mdako' in Swahili. And it was my incredibly good luck to have a real model railway with a wind-up train and stations. My friends and I spent many exciting hours pretending we were conductors and engineers running that train, stopping it at stations and changing the tracks.

At certain times of the year we would all go to a lovely country house about four miles along the coast from Zanzibar Town, near Mtoni Palace. Built in the early nineteenth century by Sayyid Said the Great, Mtoni Palace was named after a stream that was diverted to run through the ground floor of the house and on into beautiful fountains in the gardens before flowing to the sea. Set back from the shore in a lush grove of palm and mango trees amid breath-taking scenery, Mtoni, the largest of Sayyid Said's palaces, accommodated a household of more than one thousand people and was famous for its magnificent Turkish and Persian baths.*

*Based on Ruete, Emily, *Memoirs of an Arabian Princess,* Gallery Publications, Zanzibar, 1998, p 1-3.

This picture of Sayyida Salme, daughter of HH Sayyid Said bin Sultan, Ruler of Oman and Zanzibar, hangs in the Palace Museum in Stone Town. Sayyida Salme's book, *Memoirs of an Arabian Princess from Zanzibar*, details life at Mtoni and the other palaces of her father in Zanzibar during the late 1840's and early 1850's.

Dr Patricia Groves

Ruins of Sayyid Said's Palace at Mtoni

H Destro

The old mosque at Mtoni

Khalid's spacious country house at Mtoni was built into a hillside overlooking the sea. As soon as we arrived, a man was sent to the village to buy sardines which would be hastily boiled with butter and rice and put on the ground in the front yard to attract dogs. As children, we thought it amazing that all the stray dogs would collect in the yard at the precise spot where the food was about to be placed, without being called. There would be young and old dogs yelping and jostling each other to devour the sardines. With so much sudden action, this was always an exciting start to our holidays, and we liked the fact that the small dogs had their own dish.

Sayyid Khalid's sister, Sayyida Fatma told me that these dogs were the best guards, better even than human beings, because, having filled their stomachs, they wanted to express their gratitude and therefore took care to protect the property. At night, they would spread out around the building, each dog at a strategic location as if he were a guard on duty. We discovered that, if anybody approached the house at night, all the dogs would surround the intruder, barking and muscling in to attack him. With all the noise and commotion, the household would wake up, and the intruder would be forced to leave.

During our holidays at Mtoni, we would occasionally walk a short distance to the grave of the highly respected scholar, Sheikh Nasser bin Jaad Al Kharusi, said to have been brought from Oman to Zanzibar by the illustrious Sayyid Said bin Sultan (1804-1856) to be his personal advisor on religious affairs. Sheikh Nasser was buried near the site of Mtoni Palace and its mosque.

Although Mtoni Palace has long been in ruins, the mosque that Sayyid

Said constructed nearby still exists today, right on the beach. The beautiful design of the double, or once-echoed, *mihrab* (prayer niche facing Mecca) for which the Mtoni mosque is notable was made in a traditional Omani style.

My youth was, of course, not all holidays and adventures - school was a central part of my life. It might seem strange, but the truth is that I genuinely enjoyed my school days, and, like my father, took my studies seriously. People are always an important part of the equation, and there were several teachers and authority figures who made an impression on me. For example, I vividly recall Sheikh Abdulla Mohammed Al Hadhrami at Mnazimoja, Principal of the Secondary School, an imposing figure who always stood in the hall first thing in the morning when we went to recite prayers before class. Sheikh Abdulla was a very strict principal, a true disciplinarian preoccupied with authority and how it was administered. He was a man who liked to see things done properly, without a hitch.

I am sure that Sheikh Abdulla's influence helped me and some of my classmates to lead more disciplined lives than we would otherwise have led. In our juvenile way, we also found Principal Abdulla very funny. He used to get very angry with any student who waved hello at him while he was riding his bicycle, because, for some reason, he could not raise his hand to reply without the bicycle wobbling!

We thought nothing of relaxing with one hand on the handlebars and waving to all our friends with the other, whereas Sheikh Abdulla considered this practice to be very dangerous. The Principal tried not to let his students distract him from the road straight ahead and actually suspected that they might be deliberately trying to make him fall off his bicycle! In hindsight, I feel proud of the fact that we never felt tempted to make fun of him. Apparently his emphasis on discipline had an effect even outside of class.

As a teacher, Principal Abdulla was very keen on the history of Zanzibar, especially as it relates to the different rulers. In his role as headmaster, Sheikh Abdullah would always come to the exam hall to give us advice. Time and again he would recite an old Arab proverb, which I remember to this day - *"In exams, a person is either honoured or humiliated. Therefore, it is important to take time to think seriously about your answers".*

Every year, a dentist on rota came to our school to check our teeth. Two of my classmates were told by the dentist that they needed to go to the hospital for dental treatment. At the thought of the hospital, the students in question were so scared that they ran away! The dentist looked out the window and saw the two boys running away at top speed, so he rushed into the yard calling their names! Of course this only made them much more frightened of dentists.

In the course of my secondary school education I came across many different teachers, each with their own unique personalities and idiosyncrasies. They kept us incredibly busy with the usual subjects like history, mathematics and science - on top of having to study Arabic, Swahili and English. I remember that the English language teacher would come to my house to give me private lessons. Of course, Qu'ranic studies were highly important, and some of us would go to the teacher's house for extra lessons on the Holy Qu'ran.

Although we were heavily loaded with homework, we made time for sports. We all played cricket and football and often went swimming. I was very fortunate to have the opportunity to go horseback riding regularly. I also played a lot of tennis.

Our headmaster, Dr Hollingsworth, was a teacher with a great personality. He took a keen interest in all his students and was another strict disciplinarian who would not accept any nonsense. He cared enough about each one of his students that he kept individual records. If Dr Hollingsworth was not satisfied with a student's work or behaviour, he monitored the student's background and home life and would make positive interventions where appropriate. Eventually he was offered a higher post in the Department of Education. Surprisingly, Dr Hollingsworth rejected the offer because he preferred to teach, declaring that students were truly his main interest.

Many young people who were educated under Dr Hollingsworth's supervision became very successful, going on to study abroad and graduating from university. They all remembered Dr Hollingsworth with admiration and gratitude because of his excellent classes and good advice. It is fair to say that he had a significant impact on the development of Zanzibar through the generations of children he taught, many of whom later became influential.

When the time came for Zanzibar's independence, the good man was already retired and living back home in England. Most of the ministers of the new government were Dr Hollingsworth's former students. They sent him an invitation and air ticket to attend the celebrations, but Dr Hollingsworth declined as he was by then too old to travel.

Many years later, when I was in London, I phoned Dr Hollingsworth, asking for an appointment to pay him a visit. He invited me to come for tea at his club, and I was delighted to accept. Even though it had been many years since we met and we were out of our original context, Dr Hollingsworth and I related to each other in the same old way – with me sometimes dissenting. My old teacher obviously remembered that I was somewhat argumentative, as he told me that he thought I hadn't changed much. I said that he hadn't changed much either. I don't know whether he liked this comment or not!

Naturally, it was not only teachers and school authority figures who influenced me in my youth. Family always has a strong effect in the shaping of character and attitudes - and this was particularly true of my family. They were part of the Al Busaidi clan that had become the ruling dynasty of both Oman and Zanzibar; thus I was fortunate to grow up among the significant figures of the day.

Saud bin Ahmed Al Busaidi as a young man in Zanzibar, 1930

Chapter 7
Royalty all around

Among the most wonderful memories of my childhood were the times that I spent with Sayyida Fatma, a lady of exceptional kindness who took great care not only of the people around her, but also the creatures. I remember her setting out dishes of water and bird seed in the garden to nurture her small winged friends. Birds of many colours would alight with a flutter of their wings, delicately sip the water and pick at the seeds before they disappeared into the trees or flew away as I watched them magically become specks in the blue sky.

I was fortunate that this kind lady loved me very much and looked upon me as her own child. I was taken to her house so often that she seemed part of the family; she was so good to me that, even as I think of Sayyida Fatma right now, I feel a warm glow of comfort and happiness.

Among the many visitors to the stately yet inviting house that Sayyida Fatma shared with her sister Sayyida Alya was my grandfather, Sayyid Hammad - a close friend of their brother Sayyid Khalid. My grandfather came to greet the royal ladies once a year during the Eid festivities, and, for me, these were always very special and meaningful occasions as they seemed to blend our two families together.

It was in part because of Sayyida Fatma that I met the most important people in our faraway East African realm, including members of the inner Royal Family. When I was old enough, Sayyida Fatma would ask me to go downstairs to greet her distinguished guests. The Sultan himself, HH Sayyid Khalifa bin Haroub, was a not infrequent visitor. I also met his first wife, Sayyida Maatuka, and the daughter of their brother, the late Sultan Hamoud. Another royal visitor was HH Sayyida Sharifa Barghash bin Said, granddaughter of Sayyid Said the Great.

When he came to the house, His Highness Sultan Khalifa was often accompanied by his good friend Sir Claude Hollis, the British Resident of Zanzibar at that time. Zanzibar had been a British Protectorate since 1890 and the British Resident, who played a major role in the governance of the Island, had dual responsibilities. His primary duty was to enact directives from Britain and to provide his British superiors with sound advice on matters of state. At the same time, he acted as Chief Minister for the Sultan of Zanzibar.

HH Sultan Khalifa bin Haroub in 1941

*Sir Alfred Claude Hollis, was British Resident of Zanzibar from 1923 to 1929. Hollis Road in Stone Town was named after him

Sayyida Fatma and Sayyida Alya thought of Sir Claude Hollis, a dignified, yet charming and very engaging gentleman of the old school, as a good friend. The feeling was mutual as Sir Claude Hollis often said how very much he enjoyed calling on the elderly royal ladies. On such occasions the atmosphere in the house seemed rather grand and ceremonial.

Sayyida Fatma and Sayyida Alya would wear a fancy version of the *burqa* or traditional face cover, decorated with golden thread and pearls. Undoubtedly, the two sisters were strikingly impressive with their large eyes emphasized by jewelled face masks. Their shoulders were covered with gorgeous shawls made of silk embellished with gold embroidery and delicate tassels. I believe that the tasselled silk shawls were inherited from their grandfather, Sayyid Said the Great. After Sir Claude Hollis retired and returned to his home in England, he sent us a delicious fruit cake and special Christmas card every year.

Among other notable guests who visited us was Olga Said Ruete who had come from Germany to see her Zanzibari relatives. Miss Olga was the granddaughter of Sayyida Salme, author of the famous book, *Memoirs of an Arabian Princess from Zanzibar*. Sayyida Salme was one of the daughters of Sayyid Said the Great; and it was fascinating to meet this lovely young woman as a European great-granddaughter of the illustrious Sultan.

And then there was HH Sayyid Abdulla bin Khalifa, son of the Sultan and a great favourite of Sayyida Fatma and Sayyida Alya. When Sayyida Fatma introduced me to Sayyid Abdulla, she asked him to look upon me as his younger brother. So, Sayyid Abdulla would often invite me to go on outings with him.

Sayyid Abdulla was greatly interested in sports and this suited me very well. We formed a team known as the Palace Football Team and had our own pitch at Kidongo Checkundu. Once we played a match against an outside team who came determined to win. In the extremely tense last moments of the final game when the score was tied and all the spectators were holding their breath, it happened that a very fast ball was coming at me from a difficult angle, just as I was near the goal.

I had to gather courage, act quickly, and bounce the ball off my head in the direction of the goal. Luckily, I scored — and it was the winning goal! There was much jubilation with hearty congratulations for me as the declared hero of the game. Of course I felt proud, especially since I was the youngest player on the team.

As we were fortunate to have a polo club, Sayyid Abdulla and I would often go horseback riding together and practice for polo. The first time I rode a horse, I was not long in the saddle before being thrown to the ground with a sudden hard thud. Fortunately, I landed on grass and thus escaped injury. The fall just made me all the more determined to continue the sport. After some time, I became adept at polo and developed a huge interest in the equestrian world.

In the late 1930s there was an event of great significance in our family history. My sister, Sayyida Nunuu, married the Sultan, HH Sayyid Sir Khalifa bin Haroub bin Thuwaini. My sister was a popular, out-going and lively person, very fond of socializing and meeting people of all kinds. She was a highly accomplished person with great expertise in organizing social events and knew exactly how to treat the many guests who came to pay their respects to the Sultan. In fact, Sultan Khalifa, who understood very well the value of personal diplomacy, often took guests upstairs to the ladies' quarters to meet my sister. And sometimes, since they were an exceptionally devoted couple who adored doing things together, the Sultan would take Sayyida Nunuu sailing with him on the *Sultana*.

Even for the elaborate Eid festivities, my sister would arrange the celebrations herself - never leaving this prime task to the Private Secretary. After Eid prayers in the local mosque, the Sultan would invite everyone to a reception at the Palace. The guests numbered well into the hundreds. Entertaining so many guests required careful planning, and, Sayyida Nunuu would take great pains to ensure that everything ran smoothly. She always worked to a strict time schedule, a regimen which was important because there were always VIP guests with appointments to meet the Sultan in his office after the reception.

Receptions were conducted according to a certain protocol. As soon as guests from various regions and heads of different communities arrived at the Palace, attendants would guide them to the Grand Hall. Once all were seated, the Sultan entered the Grand Hall, and everyone would stand up as a gesture of respect to His Highness. When all were seated, three manservants immaculately dressed in white dishdashas and embroidered black waistcoats would begin the food service. Carrying large trays laden with sumptuous Arabian delicacies such as halwa and baklava, they served the many rows of seated guests with skilful precision.

After Omani coffee was served, servants brought bottles of perfume for the guests to sample. Fragrant rosewater was sprinkled on everyone who nodded assent. Meanwhile, the air was perfumed with the enchanting fragrance of burning bukhur, a luxurious incense powder made of an exotic mixture of aromatic ingredients such as oud, floral oils, ambergris, spices and fragrant woods. These rituals of traditional Omani hospitality lasted about half an hour, after which the Monarch would leave his seat and stand at the foot of the grand staircase where he graciously shook hands with each departing guest.

It was evident that the people of Zanzibar admired Sultan Khalifa and saw him as a great man. While maintaining his royal dignity, the

Sultan was remarkably personable and friendly with a natural sense of humour. Sayyid Khalifa had the knack of making others feel at ease and always spared time for his people, with a pleasant word or amusing remark for each and every one who came to pay their respects, even when this meant standing for many long hours. Equally relaxed and eloquent whether he was talking to a royal personage, a politician, a child or a servant, Sultan Khalifa knew how to relate to people from all walks of life.

One of Sultan Khalifa's great gifts was an excellent memory. I recall a story about a reception in England when the Sultan asked to see a particular Lord whom he had met only once, in London, many years earlier. The Lord in question was present and came forward to meet the Sultan. Both men were keen sportsmen and conversed at some length about this common interest, just as they had before. The Sultan had remembered in detail their previous conversation - to the great surprise of the Lord and of all those present.

Royalty all over the world tend to own fine horses and many are fond of equestrian pursuits. Sultan Khalifa's love of horses stemmed no doubt from his Omani heritage in which the Arabian horse is a symbol of courage and loyalty. With a pedigree dating back many thousands of years, the Arabian was bred by the Bedouin to withstand desert conditions. Selection also favoured horses that were quick to learn and companionable. They had to be strong and fast for raiding and war. Also bred for beauty, the Arabian is characterized by high tail carriage, an arched neck, a concave profile, and a wedge-shaped head with a finely-chiselled face, a broad forehead and large eyes.

According to Bedouin mythology, Allah created the Arabian horse from the four winds - to be as fast in pursuit as in flight. One of the glories of the earth, the Arabian was thought to fly without wings and to bring both riches and good fortune. It seemed just such a blessing when two Arabian horses, a stallion and a mare, arrived in Zanzibar on a monsoon dhow from Oman. The most beautiful horses I had ever seen, they were a gift for HH Sayyid Khalifa. The handsome stallion with a dark chestnut brown coat was called Dahmani, and the beautiful red-brown mare, Kihele. The two Arabians, the only such fine horses in Zanzibar, were greatly admired by everyone who saw them.

Kihele, had splendid features, her fine head distinguished by a white stripe, her jaw delicate in form. Dahmani was a true four-footed aristocrat, a proud creature of compelling beauty. He always held his head aloft, as if smelling fresh air; and his raised tail seemed to emphasize how alert he was. Here was a powerful horse with strong, well-sculpted muscles visible in contour all over his silken body.

This spirited Arabian was prone to galloping at high speeds; and was bound to misbehave at times. The harness which controlled ordinary horses was useless on Dahmani, for, when this horse started galloping, he was a force to be reckoned with. Dahmani would become incredibly energised and would not slow down, regardless of how much the rider pulled in the reins – that is until one of our friends, Sheikh Adullah bin Humeid Al Harthy, designed a special harness to control this willful horse and Dahmani was forced to relinquish his arrogance.

When I was out riding early one morning with Prince Abdulla and others, Dahmani went into a rage because he wanted to gallop beside Kihele and my horse was in the way. All of a sudden, Dahmani charged at me and my horse! He literally reared up onto my horse. I was left hanging on for dear life as my horse ran away as fast as he could – so frightened was he of Dahmani.

Eventually I fell off, sustaining a wound on one side of my back. Fortunately, as it was rather cold that time of year, I was wearing a thick jacket. Looking at the damage to my jacket I could see that it had protected me from

49

more serious injury. I had no choice but to return on foot in badly torn clothes. An old African woman who had noticed us proudly racing past her on horseback now saw me walking back in a sorry state.

Once, as we were returning to the stables at a gallop on soft ground, Dahmani refused to stop. Fearing the horse would run onto the tarmac road where he would be endangered by vehicles or cause an accident, Sayyid Abdulla threw himself off. It is said that a good horse knows and loves its rider and will not abandon him, whatever happens. Dahmani promptly came back, although rather haughtily, to his rider. How quick and clever of Prince Abdulla!

When Sayyid Khalifa was in his prime, he enjoyed horseback riding immensely and played a lot of polo. He took a special interest in each of his horses. Very often he would order that the two Arabians be brought to the Palace so that he could stroke them and feed them sugar or carrots. In this way, the animals and their owner became very close.

Riding was another shared pastime of Sultan Khalifa and Sayyida Nunuu. It was wonderful and somewhat touching to see the royal pair riding together - the Sultan on the stallion; and my sister on the mare.

But this idyllic life was soon to change as the drums of war once again sounded throughout Europe and would rapidly spread. The Second World War had a huge impact on Zanzibar, even though the Island was thousands of miles away from the eye of the storm. Once shipping was interrupted and food became scarce, it was impossible to maintain the Riding Club. When it became apparent that the horses were suffering from malnutrition, all but Dahmani and Kihele were sold to Kenyan farmers who had the means to look after them.

Dahmani and Kihele then came under the care of Sayyid Jamshid, son of Prince Abdulla, and grandson of Sultan Khalifa. Jamshid had inherited the family love of horseback riding and was very good at it. The Prince was delighted to come to the rescue of these noble horses and they flourished under his care. After the Revolution, the horses stayed at Kibweni Palace, but were comparatively neglected by the new regime and no doubt missed their royal riders.

When later a Jordanian Princess came to visit Zanzibar, a guide took her to see the two famous Arabian horses. She admired their beauty, but deplored the circumstances in which she found them. The Princess was quoted in an Egyptian newspaper as remarking that she pitied the lovely horses when she saw them downhearted and miserable, their days of glory over.

Three generations of royalty (1950) from left to right –
Sayyid Mohammed; Sayyid Abdullah bin Khalifa, the heir apparent;
HH Sultan Khalifa and his grandsons, Sayyid Jamshid and Sayyid Haroub

HRH Princess Margaret of Great Britain, alighting from
HH Sayyid Khalifa's Daimler in front of the Fort in Stone Town

HH Prince Abdulla bin Khalifa Al Busaidi with HRH Princess Margaret (October 1956)

Sultan Khalifa's love of sports was well-known in the region. Football was popular in his era, with tournaments held in various countries on a rotational basis. When the time came during the East African finals for Zanzibar to host a tournament, it was incredibly exciting as people flocked to the games and royal guests and important dignitaries arrived from the mainland. Chief among the VIPs invited by Sayyid Khalifa, was King Kabaka Muteesa II of Uganda, cousin of my friend Prince Badru. The King came to the Island on a private aircraft with a sizable royal entourage.

His Highness the Sultan invited King Kabaka to dine with him each evening. As Chief Courtier, I was responsible for the King's comfort - to ensure that everything went smoothly for him. I would accompany the King to the Palace every night for a splendid royal dinner. Afterwards, I would take the King back to his residence. It was a great compliment when I later visited Uganda to see my friend, Prince Badru, that King Kabaka invited me to his palace.

The most exciting royal event in Zanzibar in my day was the state visit of Her Royal Highness, Princess Margaret of Great Britain, to Zanzibar during her tour of East Africa in 1956. This was some time after I had returned from Oxford. The provincial administration where I was a high official was asked to ensure that the visit of Her Royal Highness Princess Margaret was a successful one, and so I was intimately involved. I attended the banquet held at the Palace in honour of the Princess and was asked to sit with her on the verandah of the Palace during the traditional Zanzibari entertainment that was arranged for her.

Entering the Palace grounds through one gate and exiting through another, eighty colourful performers in their feather-plumed headdresses danced through the courtyard for the pleasure of the Princess. It was my remit to describe the different dances to Her Royal Highness as the performers passed by. Wearing long skirts in bright patterns and adorned with a profusion of jangling bangles and colourful African jewellery, the dancers moved to the rhythm of the drums. It had been arranged, and those concerned given the instruction, that each dance troupe should perform for no more than ten minutes.

HRH Princess Margaret was enthralled with the exotic performances, and particularly liked one dance, the *Kunguiya*, known as the 'Umbrella Dance' where graceful dancers twirled their umbrellas to the mesmerizing sound of the African flute and the rhythmic beating of drums. When the drums stopped, the dancers lifted their beautiful umbrellas to form a kind of pyramid. Holding their heads high, they gazed directly at HRH Princess Margaret. So impressed was the Princess that she asked for a repeat performance! Unfortunately, this was not possible, as the show had to go on – and the stream of dancers continued unabated. I must say that the entire event was utterly entrancing - not just spectacular, but glorious.

Sayyida Nunuu walks beside HRH Princess Margaret
15th October 1956

HH Sayyid Barghash bin Said, Sultan of Zanzibar (1888)

A white concrete arch with beautiful arabesque decoration was erected in honour of the visit of HRH Princess Margaret near the seashore and the gorgeous Silver Jubilee Gardens that commemorated the 25th Anniversary of Sultan Khalifa's enthronement. When the Princess visited her arch and the gardens in 1956, she planted a tree that can be seen today - a huge, leafy canopy covered with creepers.

Life in Zanzibar was such that the habits and goings-on of the Royals were as well known to the public as they are today under the peering eyes of the modern press. There were many fascinating stories about Zanzibar's Royals in my day and in times past. I found it interesting that the old stories were relished as much as the new. The most famous and long-remembered royal figure was the first Omani ruler of Zanzibar, Sayyid Said bin Sultan, known as Sayyid Said the Great, who was born circa 1791 and reigned from 1804 until he died in 1856. From his seat as the Ruler of Oman (then known as 'Muscat and Oman'), Sayyid Said set out to build a commercial empire based on trade in the Indian Ocean Rim. In 1840, to capitalize on his by then thriving trading dominion in East Africa, he established a second capital in Zanzibar.

As was the custom for Arab monarchs in times past, Sayyid Said had more than one wife as well as many concubines who altogether bore some thirty-six children. Among the most notable of the royal issue were Sayyid Majid, who became Sultan of Zanzibar in 1856 when his father died and the Sultanate was split; Sayyid Thuwani who acceded to the throne of Oman, also in 1856; Sayyid Barghash who succeeded his half brother Sayyid Majid as Sultan of Zanzibar in 1870; and Sayyida Salme (1844-1924) who is celebrated because of her fascinating book, *Memoirs of an Arabian Princess from Zanzibar.*

There is a story that my grandfather would tell about Sayyid Majid falling seriously ill when he was a young teenager living with the family at the palace in Stone Town. When the worrying news reached his father at Bait Mtoni, a country palace further north on the coast, the Monarch went straight down to the shore, pushed a small rowing boat into the ocean and rowed unaccompanied all the way to Zanzibar Town, a distance of several kilometres. When Sayyid Majid recovered, the Sultan rowed back to Mtoni. Sayyida Salme, a young girl who adored her father and was concerned about the exertion involved, apparently told him that he should not have taken such a risk, and especially not alone, as he was no longer a young man.

Sayyid Said was extremely fond of Barghash (1837-1888), a lively, intelligent child in whom the Sultan said he saw himself as a young boy. My grandfather told me some unforgettable stories about Sultan Barghash bin Said, the third Omani ruler of Zanzibar following in the footsteps of his father, Sayyid Said, and succeeding his older brother, Sayyid Majid. It was Sayyid Barghash's father who had built the capital,

Zanzibar Town, into an impressive royal seat of power with beautiful architecture and a grand demeanour. HH Sayyid Barghash carried on the tradition, laying out a new infrastructure and erecting a number of impressive monuments, including Bait Al Ajaib, the House of Wonders.

Sayyid Barghash had a reputation as a very strong ruler, but impulsive. He was a man who would often lose his temper. Although he enjoyed absolute power, Sultan Barghash sometimes overstepped the mark. One such incident was when he almost interfered with court in session. In Sayyid Barghash's time, the Sultan's palace consisted of many interconnected buildings with overhead passages. At each entrance to a passageway, a guard stood on duty. One day when Sayyid Barghash was wandering through the Palace, he found himself on an inner verandah that overlooked the Law Courts. As the courts were in session, Barghash stood listening to the proceedings. Suddenly, in a loud, commanding voice, the Monarch called down to the Magistrate.

The Magistrate raised his eyebrows in surprise and looked up at Sayyid Barghash who then asked a question about the case. Incensed by this intrusion, but showing great restraint, the Magistrate answered the question put to him by the Monarch. He then calmly asked Sayyid Barghash if he would like to come down and take his place in court. It was a rather courageous response which could have been considered foolhardy, even insolent; and might have resulted in the Magistrate's dismissal or perhaps worse. However, Sayyid Barghash covered his face with his hands, realizing it would have been a rather serious breach of protocol to interfere in court proceedings.

Sayyid Barghash was known to be very fond of food. Every meal was a lavish affair with a stunning array of dishes. As the Sultan enjoyed cultural activities and liked to be entertained at meals, he imported a group of Turkish musicians for that purpose. During dinner, the musicians would play wonderful Arabian and Oriental music on the tabla, oud and qanoon. The performers lived on the palace grounds and gave lessons to aspiring local musicians. Hence they were responsible for introducing Arab music to Zanzibar.

During his reign (1870-1888), Sayyid Barghash encouraged farmers to plant an abundance of clove trees and develop new plantations to increase the agricultural income of the Island, since the trade in cloves was highly lucrative. At the same time, the British were putting a great deal of pressure on the Sultan to pass and implement anti-slavery laws. As the clove industry is labour intensive, farmers were clamouring for more slaves to meet the demand for increased production with high profit margins to sustain the local economy.

This posed a serious dilemma for Sultan Barghash - should he meet the pressing needs of his people, or bow to abolitionist pressure from the British? Barghash apparently said: *"I see there are two spears, one on my left and one on my right. Which one should I choose to strike me?"*

It was Sultan Barghash who gave Dar es Salaam its name, meaning Haven of Peace. When Sayyid Barghash visited that city, he was attracted by the beauty and peace of an inlet facing the harbour. My maternal great-grandfather owned a plot of land at the entrance to the harbour and had built a grand house there. It is possible that Sultan Sayyid Barghash stayed in my great-grandfather's house when he visited Dar es Salaam. While I was working in Dar es Salaam as Assistant Wali I noticed that the large, imposing house was still standing, although no longer in our family's possession.

When Sultan Barghash grew older he was unwell and quite weak. One day, while on the veranda of the Palace, the Sultan saw a labourer carrying a large gunny sack of rice on his back. Despite the extreme weight of his burden, the man was almost running along the road. Sayyid Barghash was tremendously impressed with the man's strength.

On impulse, he called the guards to summon the labourer to the Palace. The poor man was literally trembling with fear as he stood before the great Sultan of Zanzibar in his opulent palace. The Monarch's stern dark eyes stared intently at the labourer. His Highness did not speak for several minutes. Silence can be deadly with minutes passing like hours and the labourer was anxiously worrying about what he might have done wrong and what his punishment would be.

Then Sayyid Barghash spoke as if announcing the results of a formal deliberation, *"I wish I had your strength. I would give you half of everything I own, if I could only have your strength."* The Sultan instructed his aide to give the quivering labourer a good amount of money, and sent the lucky man on his way.

In the hope of improving his health, and on the advice of his medical team in Zanzibar Town, Sayyid Barghash made the long journey to Oman where he bathed in the waters of the hot springs of Bausher which were believed to have healing powers.

Today, the most well-known tales of royal life in nineteenth-century Zanzibar are those of Sayyid Barghash's half-sister, Sayyida Salme as recorded in her now famous book, *Memoirs of an Arabian Princess from Zanzibar,* written in 1886. One of the most poignant stories in the book is that of the little Princess waiting for her father, Sayyid Said to return from his last voyage abroad.

Sayyida Salme and other members of the Royal Family in Zanzibar waited patiently for three years. When finally in 1856, news arrived of Sayyid Said's imminent return, *"Sayyid Majid and his retinue took two cutters, and, battling heavy seas, which threatened to swamp them at*

*Ruete, E, *Memoirs of an Arabian Princess from Zanzibar,* Gallery Publications, Zanzibar, 1998, p. 75

any moment" *, went out to meet the Sultan's fleet, but were not seen again that night. Strangely, guards surrounded the Palace and everyone was locked in. Princess Salme and those around her had a feeling of foreboding, but did not imagine the dreadful news that awaited them.

When morning came, the fleet was sighted at anchor in the harbour. Shockingly, all the vessels were flying black flags. At first Princess Salme, only twelve years old, could not fathom that her father had died onboard. Royal to the core, Sayyida Salme does not dwell on her own pain and sorrow, instead she thinks of the greatness of her father and his legacy with the people: *"The general mourning on his death proved how sincerely he had been loved by all. Black flags hung from every house, and even the smallest hut fastened up a piece of black stuff."* *

It was Barghash who ordered guards to surround his father's palace as well as Majid's palace - in the hope of snatching the throne by fast and forceful action, but the attempted coup failed. That morning, Majid, the elder of the two brothers, proclaimed himself Sultan.

A further power struggle ensued in which the British were understood to have played a hand, as factions of the Royal Family contended for dominion over Sayyid Said's far-flung trading empire. The ultimate result was that Oman and Zanzibar became two separate Sultanates. Sayyid Said's third son, Sayyid Thuwaini, was declared Sultan of Muscat and Oman, while his sixth son, Sayyid Majid, became Sultan of Zanzibar.

Three years later Sayyida Salme lost her mother in a cholera epidemic, but bravely carried on with life in the Palace until she fell in love with Rudolph Heinrich Ruete, a young German businessman from Hamburg living in Zanzibar as representative of a mercantile firm. An interesting

* Ibid, p. 77

footnote is that our old maid, Zohra, apparently a confidante of Sayyida Salme, was one of the very few people who knew that the enamoured young Princess was planning to elope with the handsome foreigner who had won her heart. When Princess Salme took this extremely unconventional step, her life was forever changed.

HH Sayyida's Salme's tale is a tragic one; it is also a story of nobility and courage. After a few years of happiness, Sayyida Salme's husband was killed in a tram accident and she was left alone in a foreign country with three small children. The young Royal showed great courage – not once in the more than two hundred pages of her memoirs does she complain of the often cruel fate with which she had to contend.

These are only some of the fascinating stories of royal life in Zanzibar in the past two centuries, but they give a flavour of times that, in retrospect, seem to be the stuff of legends.

Sayyida Salme (Emily Ruete) in later years.

62

Chapter 8
Tales of brave men among our ancestors

I was inspired not only by the great personages of my era, but also by legendary truths about my ancestors. It was from Grandmother Aisha that I learned something of the maternal side of our family history. Her husband, my grandfather, Suleiman bin Hamed, had been the Wali or Governor of Mogadishu. Because of the political situation, Grandmother Aisha's family had experienced difficult times in Mogadishu, and they were often in grave danger.

And so it was that my grandfather Suleiman decided to send his family to live in the relative safety of Zanzibar. He planned to return to Zanzibar later, but unfortunately this did not come to pass. When the Italians invaded Mogadishu, they would not allow my grandfather to leave, as his local knowledge along with his superb political and diplomatic skills in dealing with both people and situations were invaluable to them – and thus he was commandeered to help the Italians govern.*

My maternal grandfather Sayyid Sulieman bin Hamed who had settled in Lamu, served in the highly demanding position of Wali of Mogadishu, Merka, Benadir and Barawa. My grandmother described her late husband as an impressively strong and powerful man with a reputation for exceptional competence. In a dangerous era with incessant wars between the tribes, as Governor, my grandfather had to contend with challenges of the highest order. Sayyid Suleiman risked his life every day as he travelled around the country putting down rebellions and trying to keep the peace.

* This is recorded in Cassanelli, Lee, 'The Struggle for Land in Southern Somalia – The War behind the War', Westview Press, Boulder, Colorado, 1996.

Sayyid Suleiman came from a line of distinguished Omani settlers in East Africa. It is known that my maternal great grandfather, Sayyid Abdullah bin Jaad bin Khalaf bin Said bin Mubarak Al Busaidi, emigrated from Oman to Zanzibar in 1746 at the order of the Imam, Ahmed bin Said bin Mohammed bin Khalaf bin Said Al Mubarak. At that time there was internecine conflict among the tribes, and Sayyid Abdullah's appointment as General-Governor of East Africa was meant to quell the deadly clashes.

For me as a young man with a great interest in history, it was exciting to discover that, in 1824, my paternal great-grandfather, Sayyid Hammad bin Ahmed bin Hammad Al Busaidi, led an assault on the Governor of Pate, General Mubarak bin Hamed bin Mohammed Al Mazrui, an old enemy of the Al Busaidi regime. Sayyid Said the Great had sent 4,000 troops and 30 ships to Pate, an island off the Kenyan coast near Lamu, belonging to Kenya. In the fierce battle that followed, the Governor surrendered, but then craftily made an escape to Mombasa where he knew he could find support.

When my great-grandfather and his troops entered Pate, they were welcomed by the people. Later, my great-grandfather and his men marched on Pemba to displace the Governor, Sheikh Suleiman Ali Othman Al Mazrui, scion of the clan that, from the eighteenth to the twentieth century, ruled over certain areas of East Africa, particularly Kenya - and violently opposed the Al Busaidi rulers of Zanzibar. The Mazruis were a clan of Omani descent who had arrived in East Africa earlier than the Al Busaidis.

Sayyid Hammad bin Ahmed and his men won the battle for Pemba, laying claim to the island in the name of Sayyid Said bin Sultan. Under my great-grandfather's leadership, Siyu and Mombasa were also conquered. These important victories, all under the leadership of one man, amounted to a feat of major proportions

Dignitaries aboard a British Warship in Zanzibar
Front row, left to right: 2nd-Sheikh Abdulla bin Suleiman Al Harthi; 3rd-Sayyid Hammad bin Ahmed Al Busaidi; 4th-Sayyid Salim bin Kindeh Al Busaidi; 5th-The British Resident, Sir Alfred Claude Hollis

My father's family also has a long history in Zanzibar. When my grandfather, Sayyid Hammad, came to Zanzibar in the late nineteenth century, he was following in his father's footsteps, as my paternal great grandfather, Sayyid Hammad bin Ahmed Al Busaidi, had travelled to East Africa in the early nineteenth century, during the reign of the

Front row continued, left to right:
7th-HH The Sultan; 9th-Sayyid Ahmed bin Salim Al Busaidi; 10th-Sayyid Seif bin
Ahmed Al Busaidi; 11th-Seif bin Majid Al Ma'amari

illustrious Sultan Said bin Sultan. Sayyid Hammad bin Ahmed was an extraordinarily brave man and a brilliant soldier. In fact, he had been appointed Commander-in-Chief of all the Sultan's Armed Forces by Sayyid Said. Among my great grandfather's military achievements was his success at Bandar Abbas in Iran. He led the Sultan's Forces against the Bandar Abbas Rebellion, and, with his victory in that battle, earned the nickname; '*Al Samar*', which means '*The Nail*'.

Sayyid Said was very pleased with my great grandfather's efforts and remarked, *"You really nailed them!"* It was an epithet that would last for life. Over time, Sayyid Hammad bin Ahmed became famous for his sword. He fought the Portuguese and quelled rival Omani clans. As well as fighting the Mazruis, he battled against the Nabhanis who had challenged Sultan Said's rule.

The name, Al Samar, is still remembered as part of their history by old Arab residents of Zanzibar, of the coast of Kenya, and, especially, the island of Lamu. I have heard that there are some Swahili poems praising my great grandfather, 'Al Samar,' for his heroism. I wish I could find some of those poems.

My sister, Sayyida Nunuu, had always wanted to visit the grave of her famous ancestor, Sayyid Hammad bin Ahmed ' Al Samar' Al Busaidi. Her wish was finally granted in 1959, when Sultan Khalifa decided to please his wife by arranging a visit to Lamu. My sister was tremendously excited at the prospect of the visit. There would be a great deal of socialising; and, as Sayyida Nunuu wished to be hospitable to the people of Lamu, she ensured that a generous quantity of all available dried foods was packed for the journey. The departure date was fixed for the end of November 1959. Sayyida Nunuu personally took care of all the arrangements including invitations for the important dignitaries who were to be in the entourage that accompanied the Royal Couple onboard the Zanzibar Government ship, *Sayyid Khalifa*.

A large crowd had gathered at the landing site for the Royal arrival. As the island did not have a proper port or any disembarkation facilities and His Highness Sayyid Khalifa was quite an old man by that time, he decided to remain onboard ship. The Wali of Lamu and

Mr Saleh bin Hamed Al Busaidi went onboard to welcome the Royal Couple, and once the formalities were over, my sister disembarked with her entourage.

It must be recorded that His Highness Sayyid Khalifa was only the second among the Sultans of Zanzibar to pay a visit to Lamu Island. The first Sultan to visit the Island was HH Hamoud bin Mohammed bin Said bin Sultan. While Sayyid Hamoud's visit was official, Sayyid Khalifa's visit was considered unofficial. I believe the people of Lamu had not expected to see a second royal visit from Zanzibar because of certain adverse political developments in the decades since Sultan Hamoud came to the Island. They were ecstatic about the royal visit and did everything they could to assist my sister in her quest to find the grave of 'Al Samar'.

The Royal Yacht, Sayyid Khalifa

My maternal great grandfather, Sayyid Suleiman bin Ali Al Busaidi,
Wali of Mogadishu, appointed by the Sultan of Zanzibar (1880)

Skeikh Said bin Abdulla Al Kharusi, Wali of Zanzibar (1929)

Her Highness was taken by boat to Siyu on the nearby Kenyan coast where my great grandfather was buried. There was no road to speak of, nor was there an off-road vehicle available. Thick vegetation had to be cleared to pave the way for Her Highness to walk to the grave where she intended to lay a marble stone. The grave was at the precise place where our great grandfather, 'Al Samar', had been struck down and died a noble death.

When Sayyida Nunuu reached the well-maintained gravesite, she read verses from the Holy Qu'ran in an august consecration that ended with *Al Fatha* and prayers. Then a mason carefully installed the new gravestone that Sayyida Nunuu had ordered. On it was inscribed a short history of our great grandfather, Sayyid Hammad bin Ahmed Al Busaidi, explaining the honourable reason for his burial in such an inhospitable location.

HH Sayyida Nunuu with the Zanzibar Women's Auxilliary

The Sultan and my sister decided to entertain their Lamu hosts onboard ship. As the guests arrived, their Highnesses were surprised to find

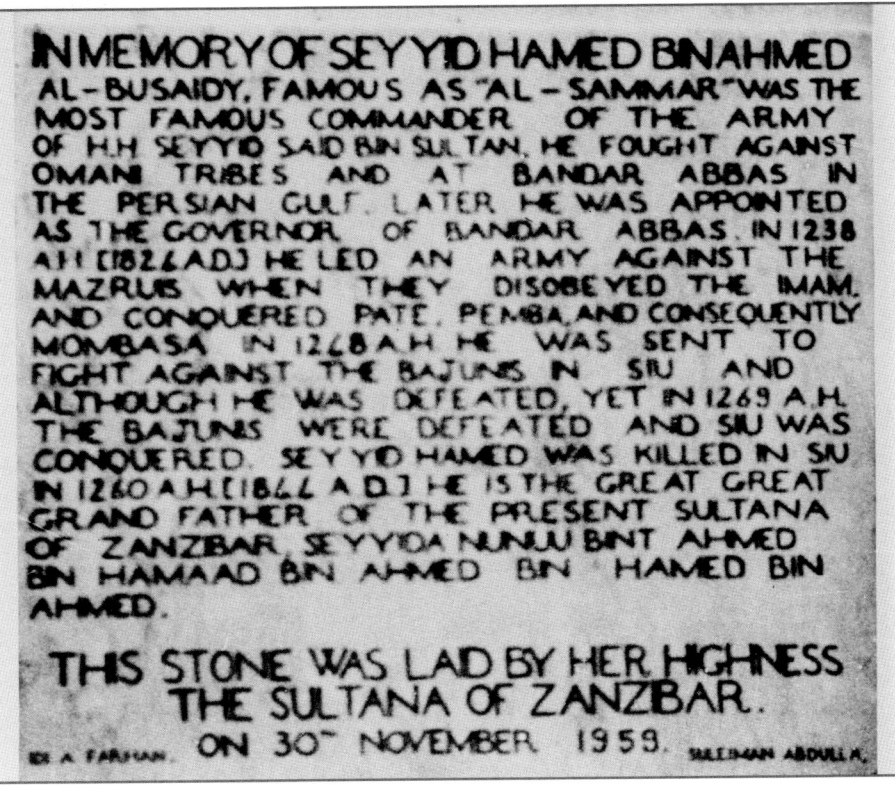

IN MEMORY OF SEYYID HAMED BIN AHMED AL-BUSAIDY, FAMOUS AS "AL-SAMMAR" WAS THE MOST FAMOUS COMMANDER OF THE ARMY OF H.H SEYYID SAID BIN SULTAN, HE FOUGHT AGAINST OMANI TRIBES AND AT BANDAR ABBAS IN THE PERSIAN GULF. LATER HE WAS APPOINTED AS THE GOVERNOR OF BANDAR ABBAS IN 1238 AH [1822AD] HE LED AN ARMY AGAINST THE MAZRUIS WHEN THEY DISOBEYED THE IMAM. AND CONQUERED PATE, PEMBA, AND CONSEQUENTLY MOMBASA IN 1248 AH HE WAS SENT TO FIGHT AGAINST THE BAJUNS IN SIU AND ALTHOUGH HE WAS DEFEATED, YET IN 1269 A.H. THE BAJUNS WERE DEFEATED AND SIU WAS CONQUERED. SEYYID HAMED WAS KILLED IN SIU IN 1260 AH [1844 AD] HE IS THE GREAT GREAT GRAND FATHER OF THE PRESENT SULTANA OF ZANZIBAR, SEYYIDA NUNUU BINT AHMED BIN HAMAAD BIN AHMED BIN HAMED BIN AHMED.

THIS STONE WAS LAID BY HER HIGHNESS THE SULTANA OF ZANZIBAR.

BY A FARHAN. ON 30" NOVEMBER 1959. SULEIMAN ABDULLA.

Photograph of the gravestone of Sayyid Hamed bin Ahmed Al Busaidi

many of the ladies of Lamu dressed in antique ceremonial clothes, which were perhaps three or four hundred years old. It was because the royal visit was of historical significance to the people of Lamu that they decided to mark the occasion by dressing in their finest attire. They looked gorgeous as well as dignified in their splendid handmade dresses. The Royal Couple wondered how the ladies of Lamu, who had few resources, managed to preserve their centuries-old clothes.

The people of Lamu were quite moved at the sight of the Royal Couple. It must have reminded them of Sultan Hamoud's visit to Lamu and the splendour and joy of that grand celebration. The story of HH Hamoud's visit had been handed down from generation to generation and this new royal visit was a chance to relive the legend. When the Royal Yacht, *Sayyid Khalifa,* left Lamu Island, hundreds of people were on the shore to wave goodbye to their Sovereign and his wife.

I still delight in the wonderful story about my paternal great-grandfather's physical strength and presence of mind. Once, when he was on an expedition deep in the jungles of the African mainland and lay resting next to a huge copper pot in the camp, a ferocious lion attacked him. With amazingly quick reflexes, Sayyid Hammad grabbed the copper pot and smashed the lion's skull.

I do not know much more about my great grandfather Hammad's life than I have related here, but I do know how he died. In the second round of fighting in 1844 my great grandfather was killed while fighting against the Bajunis. Apparently, great grandfather Hammad, a rather private man, preferred to pitch his tent some distance from his men when he travelled around the African mainland. One night, as he walked alone in the dark towards his tent, some Bajuni rebels sprang from the bushes and attacked him.

Although hopelessly outnumbered, Sayyid Hammad retaliated, injuring all his assailants with fast and accurate slices of his deadly khanjar, before falling to the ground, mortally wounded. I wish I had met him. He must have been a truly great man.

As I look back, I realize how much my childhood and youth were shaped by family life and school, as well as by something less substantial but nevertheless powerful - the legacy I inherited from outstanding people on both sides of the family. Mine was not to be an ordinary life.

HH Sayyid Abdullah bin Khalifa (1960 - 1963)

Chapter 9
The vicissitudes of life in government

While I began my career in the private sector, by far the majority of my working life was spent in government - in Tanganyika, Zanzibar, Libya and Oman. I found that the beauty of working in government in relatively small countries such as these was that I could contribute tangibly to the growth and overall development of the nation. Fortunately, in the private sector, I had acquired hands-on entrepreneurial and management skills that allowed me to sustain a dynamic approach to my work in government.

When I finished my secondary school education, I decided I would try my hand at managing the family coconut plantations. This involved supervision of the harvesting process and ensuring sales. Although my late grandfather had not done so well with the plantations, I was able to turn the business into a success. However, since it was seasonal, this work did not fully occupy my time. I felt like time was slipping through my fingers and feared I might be wasting my youth and energy. I wanted a job that could give me broader experience and the opportunity to meet different kinds of people, but I knew that a job of that kind could not be found in Zanzibar.

At that time there was massive development underway in Dar es Salaam, the capital of Tanganyika, as Tanzania was then called. Many young men were tempted to leave their native Zanzibar for jobs abroad. They dreamed of seeing the outer world in the making. Fortunately, I secured a post in Dar es Salaam as Assistant Wali or 'Deputy-Governor', reporting to Sayyid Hamed bin Saleh Al Busaidi, a man of great experience with whom I got on very well.

During the First World War, before he went into Public Administration, Sayyid Hamed was in the East African Rifles as were many young men at the time. Soon after the war, Sayyid Hamed and a number of fellow officers were sent into the Kenyan hinterland to mark the boundaries of Kenya with Tanganyika and Abyssinia. He told me that this task involved three months of rough and dangerous trekking through the bush.

In the early 1920's following the defeat of Germany in the First World War and the difficult transition from German to British rule, Sayyid Hamed served as Wali in one of the districts of Tanganyika. I discovered that he had also worked in several other provinces before he became Wali of Dar es Salaam. My mentor had a wealth of experience which was mine for the taking and from which I greatly benefited.

During the three years that I served in my post as Assistant Wali, from 1945 to 1948, I came to know and understand people from many different cultures. At that time, in the hope and exuberance of the Post World War II period, colonial peoples were starting to think seriously about gaining independence from their Imperial rulers. Already, the British Government had announced that it was going to abolish colonialism and give independence to the British African colonies.

With this declaration hanging tantalizingly in the air, many African countries started preparing for independence. Political activities were rife, with mass meetings during which inflammatory statements were made by radical would-be politicians. Framing the world in terms of 'haves' and 'have-nots', they aspired to middle class standards and coveted luxuries such as western houses and cars.

What annoyed and confused many colonial peoples was that when they asked for the promised independence, they were told that the time was not yet right. This became fodder for revolution as they felt they were being cheated. There was a widespread belief among colonials that, in spite of their promises, the British Government would not give them independence without a fight.

It seemed to me that the declaration to give the colonies independence had been premature. The British Government should first have ascertained the capability of colonial peoples to run their own governments. This mistake was surprising, since it was the British Government that had introduced education in the colonies. As the greatest imperial power of the modern era, Britain should have known better, and taken the trouble to evaluate conditions in their African colonies and determine their readiness to rise up and go forward as independent nations.

It was my firm belief that the British Government should have understood that it would have been expedient to accelerate education and training throughout their African empire before announcing their plans to disband it, so that the people they ruled were better prepared to assume the mantle of power.

In the meantime, the colonies became aggressive, demanding immediate independence. The truth is that most of the colonies were not ready to handle affairs of state and take the reins of government in their own hands. The proof of this soon emerged as chaos erupted in many of the newly liberated colonies. Unfortunately, the African people suffered immensely because of the mistakes of their leaders in attempting prematurely to govern.

However, these were changes that brought opportunities for me. In 1948, I was offered the post of *Mudir* (local Administrator) of Stone Town and replied that I would accept if a number of conditions were satisfied. Once all my requests were met, I took on this new challenge with enthusiasm and a sense of destiny in the making, for I was returning to take up a very good post in my homeland. Since I had been working in Tanganyika, which was at the time a separate country, there was no possibility of a transfer to Zanzibar, and so I had to resign.

In the following year, 1949, fortune smiled on me when I married Samira Salim Al Ma'amari. Our eldest daughter, Rayyan, was born in Zanzibar Maternity Hospital on the 5th April 1950. My wife was exceptionally well looked-after in the hospital as her aunt was a midwife of long experience and her sister was the Matron. Rayyan was a beautiful, strong baby and we were both thrilled at her arrival. Three years later on the 24th of June, 1953, our second daughter, Rawya, was born. Rayyan and Rawya were such intelligent children! We felt fully blessed when our long-awaited son, Ahmed, arrived on 23rd December 1957.

All three children attended St Joseph's, a good private school in Stone Town where studies were offered in the English language. As Samira was a teacher in the government secondary school, some people asked us why we sent our children to St Joseph's School instead of a government school. The answer was that the medium of instruction in government schools was Swahili, and our children needed to study in English, because, even before they were born, we were planning to send our children abroad for their later education. Applicants to the excellent overseas schools that we had in mind were required to be proficient in the English language.

My work kept me extremely busy. There were many challenges; in particular, I was frustrated in my determination to alter Zanzibar's post-war agricultural policy, which I knew would be detrimental to the Island's economy. During the Second World War, there had been a campaign to make Zanzibar self-sufficient in food, because the reduced shipping trade could not supply all that we needed at that time. Farmers were encouraged to grow crops in order to become self-sufficient; and I was required to journey long distances into the bush to ensure that crops were being cultivated. I would travel around in my old beige Ford, frequently stopping to traverse the fields in my inspection of the crops, as each month I had to submit a detailed report to the Government on my findings.

I must admit I became very angry after the War when the British Resident informed us that the Government of Zanzibar would begin to import agricultural goods from abroad, even though the markets of Zanzibar were full of local produce. Obviously, the British had a loyalty to the East India Company who owned the ships that transported Zanzibar's imported goods. My loyalty was with the Zanzibari farmers and retailers who could not compete with the prices of imported food. Gradually Zanzibar lost its ability to feed itself. It was a great shame, and I did not hesitate to tell senior British officials that I felt their policy was detrimental to the interests of Zanzibar.

Administrative officers had multifarious duties. Among the more interesting of these was the task of safeguarding and maintaining the ruins of Marhubi, a palace built by Sultan Barghash for his harem in the 1880's, which was accidentally burned to the ground in 1899. Marhubi was of particular interest because of its *falaj* - an ingenious water conveyance system powered by gravity, the design of which was imported from Oman. Originating in springs at Babubu, water was channelled underground by gravity and engineered to surface at Marhubi Palace where it fully met all the domestic needs of the residents. The Marhubi falaj system also included water streams coursing through channels constructed above ground and flowing abundantly into the gardens of the Palace.

At one stage prior to his ascension to the throne, Sayyid Barghash was exiled to India where he grew very fond of the delicious, plump mangoes that grow so well in the fertile gardens of that land. When he returned to Zanzibar for his enthronement, Sayyid Barghash brought back crate-loads of the best golden Alphonso mangoes. Later, Sultan

Barghash sent a ship to India to collect mango seeds and a quantity of rich Indian soil in which to grow them – hence the importance of the *falaj* irrigation system at his new palace. And so it was that mango trees from Indian seeds flourished in Zanzibar.

With a burning ambition to keep improving my ability to serve in government, in 1949, I approached the Zanzibar Department of Education for a scholarship so that I might further develop my knowledge of Public Administration. My colleague, Hilal Mohamed Al Barwani, joined me in this quest. The Department of Education had never before given scholarships to the District Administration Department. However, after careful consideration, they agreed not to block our requests, and we broke ground as the first officials from the Department of District Administration to be awarded scholarships to study in the United Kingdom.

With high expectations and a rising spirit of adventure, Hilal and I boarded a plane bound for London with a three-day stopover in Paris. I must say that it was tremendously exciting for me to be in the fabulous, faraway capital of Paris, particularly after the long journey from Zanzibar. I couldn't wait to see this marvellous city that is world famous for its historic architecture and romantic ambience.

Right after breakfast on the first morning, we set out on a one-day walking tour of the key sights, including, of course, the Eiffel Tower and the Champs Elysée. We stopped for lunch at a delightful small restaurant that we happened to come across, and, for the first time in our lives, enjoyed utterly delicious, authentic French cuisine. We returned to our hotel in the evening thoroughly charmed with all we had seen and deeply imbued with the atmosphere of *la vie Parisienne* - practically walking on air. I must however say that, in spite of our youth and high spirits, we were thoroughly exhausted!

On the second day of our visit, no doubt seeing that we were tourists, an Algerian approached us and asked if we would like to change our money into French currency at very good rate of exchange. When we said yes, the Algerian stranger asked us to count our money and tell him how much we wanted to exchange. As we began the transaction, he said, "*Be quick - the Police might arrest us because what we are doing is illegal* ".

The instant we gave the Algerian our British pounds and he gave us francs, he shouted, "*Police!*" and ran off. In seconds we realized that the man had given us less than the amount he owed us. We promptly gave chase, but the slippery Algerian had vanished into thin air. We had been robbed! To our chagrin, later at the hotel, we learned that we could have changed our money there at a much better rate.

When we landed in London, Hilal and I had difficulty walking, as our feet were blistered from walking all over Paris. Nevertheless we made it to the Commonwealth Office, where an official briefed us and suggested we go by train to Penzance in Cornwall in the southwest of England where arrangements had been made for us to study the functions of the local Borough Council.

The weather in Penzance was warm and made us feel more at home. The Borough Council had prepared a program for us. Hilal and I were allocated to different departments for a week's internship. The Borough Council was a mini-government dealing with all public services, including the police and courts. It was exciting for us to watch elected representatives of the people confidently manage all government operations without expert assistance. For them it was business as usual.

While I was observing a session in court, the police presented a case concerning a man charged with stealing from a street newspaper seller.

From time to time, the vendor would leave his stand, and during these periods, customers would simply take a newspaper, put their payment on the ground, and continue on their way. This showed that the news vendor trusted people. However, one day when the vendor was not there, a man approached the newspaper stall in a slow and deliberate manner, furtively looked around; and, thinking no one was watching, scooped up all the money on the ground and hastily walked away.

But someone from a distance saw the thief and recognized him. When the vendor came back to his stand, he was dismayed to see that all the money had disappeared. Soon the witness appeared and told the vendor what had happened. The two went off to report the crime to the police. Justice was served as the culprit was caught, arrested, found guilty, and sent to prison.

While we were in Penzance, we visited quite a number of picturesque towns in the environs - including St Just, Land's End and St Ives. We also went by boat to the Scilly Isles. Completely new and fascinating to us, these charming places left us with good memories, as did the staff of the Borough Council. Without exception, they were courteous, kind and very helpful, especially by explaining their work in ways that were easily understood. One person in particular was exceptionally hospitable - Ms June Chamberlain who, in fact, became a friend for life with our families visiting back and forth over the succeeding years. I have found that, in the best of circumstances, cultural differences between people are mutually interesting and become ties that bind.

After three months in Penzance, we were finally on our way to Oxford, the university that I had chosen with a heady sense of inspiration. Hilal Mohammed Al Barwani enrolled with me and we felt elated knowing we were pioneers together - the first civil servants from Zanzibar to go to the United Kingdom to study Public Administration. I was at Jesus College, the same college chosen by the famous British Army officer and author, TE Lawrence (1888-1935), later known as 'Lawrence of Arabia'. I relished the Oxford experience in every way, and learned a great deal.

My wife, Samira, who was still teaching in Zanzibar, applied for a scholarship to take a Bachelors Degree in English at the University of Oxford so that we could be together. Unfortunately, there was no room for Samira at Oxford, but she was offered a place at London University, which she accepted. On weekends we would go to London to visit Samira who had naturally become somewhat lonely as it is not easy at first for someone alone to adapt to a new and radically different social environment far from home. In time, Samira began to mix with students from quite a range of backgrounds and eventually made some good friends among them.

The University of Oxford exceeded my expectations as the superb educational institution that it is reputed to be. While Al Azhar University in Egypt is said to be the oldest university in the world, Oxford is the oldest university in the English speaking world, with some form of teaching evident as early as 1096 AD. As the University of Oxford evolved over the centuries, its program repertoire increased, and it seemed to me, from the vantage point of the twentieth century, that there was nothing one could not study there.

At Oxford, the doors of knowledge were, and still are, wide open. I was extremely impressed with both the quality of education and the depth of knowledge demonstrated by the professors. For example, after attending a lecture on modern agriculture, I put a question to the lecturer who unhesitatingly referred me to a page number in a certain book in the library. I fetched the book and found the answer on exactly the page indicated by the Professor.

At Oxford, students could participate in a wide variety of sports. It was plain to see from the crowded games that students were not supposed to shut themselves in their rooms with their books all the time. We were encouraged to take part in games as a way of improving our health and physical fitness. For my part, I took up cricket and rowing.

In earlier days in Zanzibar, Prince Abdulla, Said Hilal Al Bualy and I, along with a few friends, used to go fishing in a row boat; and so we became proficient at rowing. This turned out to be a good preparation for rowing at Oxford. The first race in which I participated was between Oxford and Cambridge, an event that should not be mistaken for the great annual racing competition between the two Universities, since our race was for colonial students only.

During the first training session, it was apparent that the coach did not expect to see me holding the oars in the proper fashion and rowing as effectively as I did. When he told me that I did not need to train because I already rowed very well, I protested, saying that I wanted to practice and improve my skills. I was determined to go down to the river and row as often as possible!

I was given the position second to the front oarsman, my friend, Said Saif Al Busaidi from Mombasa who was studying English. Said Saif was quite an athletic young man; and, like me, he was experienced at rowing. Our Skipper was told by the trainer that he should endeavour to keep to the landside as much as possible, to guard that advantage, never allowing the competing boat to take that position away from us.

Rowing is a unique phenomenon in that one rows with one's back toward the destination. Thus, we could not see that the Skipper was

With Rayyan and Rawya

With Samira

Left to Right - Rawya, Samira, baby Ahmed, the Author, and Rayyan

85

Graduating from Oxford

With Said Saif Al Busaidi

With a friend in the Oxford days

With Samira and Said Saif

heading us in the wrong direction out on the river, or we would have told him to steer the boat to the landside. We had no part in the steering of the boat and were totally focused on rowing as hard, fast and skillfully as we could.

It was very frustrating to discover that we were defeated in the race because of a strategic error on the part of our Captain. Maddeningly, as the Skipper directed the boat away from the land, the Cambridge team seized the opportunity, stole the best position, and cut us short. Cambridge won the race, but by a small margin. Had we stuck to the landside, we would easily have won.

There was a wonderful atmosphere at the University and most of our fellow students were quite convivial. Students often invited each other to their rooms for informal receptions so that they could get to know one another or in order to celebrate a special occasion. It was because I had such a positive experience at Oxford that when my daughter, Rawya, consulted me as to which university she should choose for her PhD, I recommended the University of Oxford.

At Oxford there were many societies, among which was an East African Society that held a meeting at the start of each year to welcome new students. When we first arrived, there was a notice on the board announcing a meeting, and all East African students were invited. Naturally, I made a point of attending. The guest speaker was Ms Marjorie Perham, a lecturer who specialized in East African Affairs. Her talk was on the history of East African slavery which, she said, was dominated by Arabs. She claimed that it was the British Government who came to the rescue and released the slaves from their chains.

When Ms Perham finished her lecture, she asked if there were any questions. I waited, but, as no one spoke, I stood up and somewhat boldly but matter-of-factly asked Ms Perham if she could please estimate the number of slaves taken from East Africa by Arabs, as opposed to the number taken by British traders to America. She said the slaves that the British sold in America were far greater in number than those taken by Arab traders.

I also asked Ms Perham about the treatment of the slaves on board British sailing ships compared with the treatment of slaves on Arabs vessels. She had to admit that the treatment of the slaves by the British on the journey to America was worse. I proceeded to question her about the treatment of slaves once they were indentured in America when they laboured night and day on farms and in mines. She agreed that it was terrible. Ms Perham could not deny these facts, because the truth about slavery was no longer a secret as many books had been published on the subject.

I simply could not understand the lecturer's reason for reminding East African students that some of their ancestors had been slaves or slave traders centuries ago. Why did she mention the Arabs in particular, all the while avoiding reference to the British who were far more active in slavery in Africa, plundering both the West and East African coasts to capture people for the American slave market?

Definitely she was aware that, during this period of darkness and ignorance in world history, slavery was practiced in many countries and was not widely regarded as wrong. Slavery was seen in a different light in that era than it is today. No wonder none of the students wanted to ask questions. I am sure they did not like to be reminded that their forefathers might have been either slaves or slave traders. Later, Ms Perham was kind enough to invite me to tea at her house where we amicably extended the discussion, and then moved on to other topics. I discovered that she had written a biography of Lord Rhodes, and, in spite of her biases, was very knowledgeable about East Africa.

At the end of our course at Oxford, just before our departure, my colleague, Hilal, and I invited our Professors to lunch. As chance would have it, I discovered during the course of the conversation that the wife of our Superintendent of Studies was the sister of William Addis who worked in Zanzibar for many years as Private Secretary to HH Sultan Khalifa. When Albert Edward, Prince of Wales, came to Zanzibar on a state visit *circa* 1935, it was said that the only woman the Prince of Wales danced with at the reception held in his honour was William Addis' wife. Obviously the Addis couple was held in very high esteem.

We soon discovered that William Addis' sister was an exceptionally kind lady. I have mentioned that my friend, the front oarsman, Said Saif Al Busaidi, was with us at Oxford. Unfortunately, one day Said Saif developed a serious fever; and, because Said Saif's landlady was afraid of catching the disease, she was very unhelpful, refusing to bring Said Saif food or assist him in any way.

Two days later, I was with friends discussing Said Saif's plight. William Addis' sister overheard the conversation and decided to take charge of the situation. Furious with the landlady, she immediately arranged for food and supplies to be sent to Said Saif. Next she personally went to see Said Saif and scolded the landlady for her ignorance and negligence.

My days at Oxford were memorable in many ways. I shall never forget some of the people I met there, especially those who became great friends, such as Ali Ahmed Al Jahadhmi from East Africa who taught Swahili to British cadets preparing for duty in Kenya. Among my other friends were two Malaysian Princes called Abdul Majid and Abdul Hamid with whom I used to go horseback riding. I also remember a Nigerian couple with a newborn baby who had an extreme reaction to the change of climate and the bitter cold. The couple stayed in a boarding house where they sat near the heater all the time, refusing to open the door - even for the maid to clean their room.

I left Oxford in 1955, returning to my work with government in Stone Town where two years later I was promoted to the post of District Commissioner for the town and its surrounding area with a total population of 17,000. My responsibilities were extensive. They included holding court and ensuring the peace and prosperity of the town's inhabitants, its security, food production, and education. I spent a great deal of time touring around, meeting with the people who lived in the town and outlying areas, listening to their complaints, sorting out disputes, resolving conflicts and making improvements. I had several *mudirs* (regional administrators) working for me, and was obliged to report to the Senior Commissioner on a regular basis.

When I came back home from Oxford, I was full of energy and enthusiasm and I tried to practice what I had learned during that short period which was, in my opinion, insufficient. I wished that it could have been longer. While at Oxford, I wrote to my Government asking them for an extension of the scholarship to allow me to study law. I was keenly interested and already had sponsorship from a lawyer with whom I had come into contact in both Zanzibar and London.

The reply from Zanzibar was negative. This was a great pity, and also ironic, because one of the positions I would later hold, as Administrative Officer, required me to study Law. Officers were empowered to hold court at the level of lower class Magistrate. It was then that I was notified that I was required to study certain parts of British law, along with Zanzibari law. I was given, I think, three years to study in my spare time, at home. I worked hard, duly mastering the relevant material, and then sat for an examination conducted by the Chief Justice, Sir John Gray. I am pleased to say that I passed and was eventually appointed as Magistrate to hold court in my district. I found magisterial work most interesting in many ways - from the point of view of legal interpretation, the exercise of judgment, decision-making and exposure to a range of people and their problems.

An appointment of equal interest was representing the Government in the town municipality. It was my duty to watch that the municipality did not transgress the law. Stone Town Municipality, like any other municipality, was empowered by the Government to make its own laws, by-laws and rules. Operations were professionally managed, with, for instance a qualified lawyer in the post of Municipal Town Clerk facilitating all legal work.

Working with British officers who were brought to Zanzibar to run the Government was very productive as well as interesting, since they were educated people, many of whom had experience in other colonial countries. I must say we learned a lot under their guidance. But, in my opinion, their education and behaviour were two quite different things. When it comes to action, I discovered that a thoughtful education does not necessarily mean a thoughtful man.

One of the senior British officers in our Public Administration Department decided to give a lecture in English. Most of those who attended were English speaking, as far as I can remember. The subject was the political progress in Zanzibar and the right of people to choose their leaders according to the party system. When the officer finished his talk, he asked for questions. As usual, when no-one responded, I thought I would take the initiative and ask a question which might be of interest to the audience.

My question was, "*What was the British Government's policy in Zanzibar?* "The officer answered by abruptly saying there was no policy and that the meeting was closed. After a few weeks, I received a letter from the officer who had given the lecture saying that he thought I was inclined to deal with politics which was not appropriate for a government official, therefore, I could retire from government service if I so wished.

That surprised me because I had put my question in good faith. I thought the officer would say that it was a good question. I imagined he would start by mentioning that the British Government's policy in Zanzibar had been, and still was, to educate the people, by opening up schools everywhere, and building hospitals and clinics throughout the country. I thought he would also say that it was their policy to supply clean water and electricity to the towns and villages and to improve agricultural output and so on.

Most importantly, I hoped finally that the British Government's policy would be to approve elections so that the people could choose their leaders by democratic means, and later they could ask for independence, just as many other countries under British administration had done. The official could have scored points by mentioning that all the progress achieved to date depended solely on the income of the state, a remarkable achievement considering that Zanzibar was a small island with less than a quarter of a million people. Moreover, as an agricultural, not an industrial country, Zanzibar depended on a rich harvest of its crops, which of course could not always be assured. What the British administration had accomplished was no small thing. If the audience had heard this, they would perhaps have better appreciated the British contribution. It was an opportunity lost.

I did not reply to the curt letter from the senior officer. Later, at the end of his career, this disappointing man left Zanzibar. Another senior commissioner was given the post. The successor was a huge improvement, especially when it came to dealing with juniors. He was a man who could see beyond ethnic barriers; moreover, he was empathetic, quite friendly, and surprisingly pleasant to work with. The new Commissioner was even prepared to listen to people, welcoming discussion and never showing displeasure when a junior asked questions. Consequently, he learned a lot as people felt they could be open with him. Certainly the new Commissioner would not have gained the intelligence he needed to do his job as well as he did, had he made himself unapproachable in the fashion of his predecessor.

Zanzibar was not without its deviants. I usually worked cooperatively with the police force, but, occasionally, we would clash. Once, when I was in a cinema, I distinctly smelled strangely obnoxious fumes. Later I found out that the fumes were from marijuana. Apparently, dried leaves were rolled up and smoked like a cigarette. I mentioned the incident in my monthly report. The British Resident immediately called the Police Chief wanting to know why no action had been taken to enforce the law regarding the use of marijuana in public places. The police then took action.

Portrait of the Author

Mombasa Government Officials, 1946
Centre figure, front row - Salim bin Khalfan Al Busaidi, Chief Wali

On further investigation, I discovered large areas where the banned substance was under cultivation and was able to pinpoint the places where it was being sold. The police swooped down on the culprits and made many arrests. The illegal brewing of alcohol was also an issue.

These were action-packed times, and as if life were not exciting enough, we went for the ultimate adventure – hunting wild game.

Chapter 10
Adventures in the wild

In the old days, I was extremely energetic and active – a young man with a passion for the sporting life. Hunting was considered one of the greatest sporting challenges of my era, and I used to love going on safari. I remember being very excited when a friend of mine in Mombasa, Mohammed Said Al Busaidi, a very keen hunter, kindly invited me to join him on a hunting expedition.

Soon I was off to Mombasa where I found Mohammed preoccupied with the administrative and logistic arrangements for the trip. Hunting licenses had to be procured from the relevant government authorities. These licenses stipulated what kind of animals could be hunted and how many. Each particular animal had its taxation, and some were more expensive to hunt than others.

First the guns were cleaned and checked; if they were found not in good working order, they had to be repaired and cleaned. The vehicles which were assembled to transport the hunters and their staff as well as all the necessary equipment and supplies, including tents, food and water, also had to be inspected. It was particularly important to ensure that all the tires were fit for rough travel and spare parts onboard in case of malfunction or a breakdown during the long expedition. It was certainly good news to hear that some members of the group knew how to repair vehicles.

Once we were certain that everything was in order, we were ready to venture off on safari. Leaving at the crack of dawn the next morning, we travelled north toward Malindi and onwards into the bush, where we picked up an old man who lived in the wilds. The old man had knowledge of all the different animals and their seasonal migratory routes. Most hunters needed the help of a man such as this who lived among wild animals and was familiar with their habits. It was surprising how the old guide, who lived alone in a hut in the wilderness, kept himself safe from lions and elephants - and snakes too. He survived on small game, produce from his vegetable plot and tinned food from the hunters he guided.

The old man joined the safari as our guide. After a short drive through the bush, we got out and walked in silence, camouflaged in the dappled shade of trees. Our guide certainly knew what he was doing as it was not long before we sighted in the distance a herd of about two hundred antelope feeding on fresh grass. We managed to shoot one, which made a fine dinner that night for a hungry band of hunters.

We had pitched our tents on open ground and divided the group in two for the purpose of carrying out different tasks such as skinning the game, cooking, cleaning up and arranging our sleeping gear in the tents before nightfall. We wanted to go to bed early and rise at dawn so that we could catch up with the game at feeding time.

Naturally we did our best to avoid lions and elephants, but occasionally these dangerous animals would cross our path. Early one morning, we were confronted with two lions, a male and a female. They were surprised to see us, just as were we to see them. We stopped. Man and beast looked steadily at each other from a distance.

Soon the lioness disappeared into the bush, leaving her mate alone. The guide told us that the lioness would wait a while, lurking in the bush behind us, camouflaged, and would then try to take us by surprise in a lightning fast attack from the rear. He advised us to leave, so we did. In a matter of about half an hour, the lioness was spotted following us. Having by then ascertained that we were not interested in her or her mate, the stealthy hunter disappeared.

Sometime later, we shot an antelope larger than the one that made our first dinner. It is very exciting to track game in the vehicle, and then, when the animals are in sight - to venture out on foot, find a place to hide, and wait for the right moment to take aim. Animals seek pasture in herds as large as one or two hundred. I believe that herds have guard animals which look out for predators. If the guard animals see anything suspicious that might suggest lion, leopard or human beings, they signal an alert. Then the animals raise their heads, cock their ears and rapidly scan the area. In a matter of seconds, they abruptly turn and take off, running *en masse* in the same direction like a fast-moving storm in the dust. They must have a leader who signals the direction.

That night we slept in a bush camp. Fires were lit all around the camp and two men were on duty, with a changing of the guard every couple of hours. At dawn, we heard a lion roaring loudly as he approached the camp. The beast must have smelled meat. The sound grew louder and louder but, of course, we were prepared to challenge this lordly intruder. Perhaps the lion then saw the fire and the tents - or even the guards. In any case, the fierce king of the jungle suddenly changed course and disappeared into the darkness of the bush. He sensed that it was too risky to attack us.

On the third day we journeyed along the Tana River, a region full of animals attracted by the water. People who frequented the area were aware of the dangers, particularly from crocodiles and snakes. The latter were silent, hidden enemies, while large animals like lions and elephants could be seen and heard on their approach. In spite of the obvious risk, we set up camp by the river and settled in for what we hoped would be a good night's sleep. Luck was with us, as the night went by without incident and the next day we shot lots of game.

Many interesting things occur during hunting expeditions. I remember an occasion when a man from Zanzibar, who, like me, was not accustomed to detecting crocodiles, went down to the edge of the river to wash the plates after lunch. He was warned to look around for signs of the predator before kneeling down to wash the dishes.

As the man neared the water's edge, shaking with fear of crocodiles, he slipped into the river and all the plates floated away! He screamed, and his companions rushed down with their guns to rescue him from crocodiles, but, to their amazement, they could not find a single crocodile. Although relieved, the poor man was apologetic and seriously embarrassed, as hunters pride themselves on being fearless.

On one of our hunting trips, rumours reached Mamburui, a village in the region through which we had earlier passed and were using as a base, that we had shot a hippopotamus, but the rumours were unfounded. We had not even come close to killing a hippo. On our return to Mamburui, we found that elderly people had gathered to wait for distribution of the meat, as the hippopotamus is a huge animal, and it was customary to share the kill. Since there was no hippopotamus, the old people were extremely disappointed and started grumbling. They thought we were keeping the meat for ourselves.

But how could we have eaten such a big animal on our own? This didn't enter their minds. I asked why only the elderly people seemed to be so keen for the meat. The reply was that hippo meat is considered an aphrodisiac for elderly people. They were reported as saying that the young people had no sympathy for the needs of the elderly!

One night during our stop at Mamburui Village, we decided to go hunting for wild boar. With search lights attached to our foreheads, we set out in a truck, travelling some distance out of the village and disembarked at a place where there were many fields of maize. Before we left the house we had discussed the technique of hunting at night and what dangers we were likely to encounter. The briefing was particularly important for me and other new members of the hunting party. Although we had been allowed guns during daytime hunts, we were told that we would not be permitted to carry guns for the night hunt. The lead hunter instructed us to follow closely behind those who were issued guns. This disappointed and alarmed me because I felt that I could possibly be in danger and unable to defend myself, but I said nothing as I did not want to make a fuss.

Subconsciously I must have been looking for a way of defending myself, because as we were walking past the maize fields, I spotted a pole stuck in the ground as a marker between two fields, and impulsively snatched it out of the ground. After determining that it was a good, strong pole, I felt a little more secure, and walked on with some confidence - at least I was no longer both unarmed and empty-handed.

We entered the bush in the dead of night and walked stealthily along in the hush of the hour under cover of darkness. Suddenly we saw yellow eyes glowing eerily in a thicket. The lead hunter silently made a sign for us to disperse and form a half circle, facing a beast that we could not recognize. What kind of animal was it? My heart started beating fast, but I told myself to stay cool, as I had a long, hard pole in my hand, already raised and ready for action.

With a bold and menacing silence in the stillness of the night, the animal surveyed us. We did the same, while our lights shone steadily in its eyes. At the right moment, the leader of our group, Mohammed Said Al Busaidi, raised his rifle, took aim and shot. With bared teeth, the animal instantly leapt out of the thicket and headed straight towards me, the one who had no gun!

99

Instinctively, I mustered all my strength and struck the beast squarely on the head. As I heard the crash of my pole on its skull, I lost my balance and fell down on the animal. I could smell its strong musky odour and feel its warm body heat. It was a wild boar!

I then got up, not sure if the boar were dead or not. The hunters gathered around to check and they confirmed that the beast was indeed dead. Mohammed wanted to know where the bullets had penetrated the animal, but said he would determine this in good light back at the camp. The pole had served us well. First, I defended myself with it, and then, we tied the four legs to the pole; and two of us carried the dead beast back to the car.

On the way to the vehicle we were treading a footpath near the maize fields when, in the beam of the flashlight, we saw something slithering on the path. Quick as lightning, Mohammed shot at it. It was an enormous python so long that we could not tell where the head was. It was a chilling thought to realize that the python had been lying there waiting for something or someone to step on it, so that it could quickly enfold and crush the victim.

When the smoke from the gun cleared, the python had disappeared, but we didn't bother to search for it. Next morning the news reached us that farmers had found the python dead, and half its body was in an ant hole. The farmers were sorry that ants had already spoiled the skin as it would have fetched a good price in the market.

Boar hunters in Zanzibar talk about a mysterious power of the python. They say that when hunting dogs encounter a python in the bush, the snake opens its mouth and a strange smell permeates the air. As the dogs breathe the tainted air they seem hypnotized and their legs weaken. Spell-bound, the dogs crumble. On their knees, they move forward robotically, heading straight toward the waiting python! It is a most extraordinary phenomenon. Hunters know when it is about to happen because the dog's bark changes to a pitiful subdued howl. At that point, the hunter must act fast; throw a lasso around the dog's neck, and drag the dazed creature away to stop it from submitting to the deadly python.

Back at camp we began to skin the boar and discovered that the bullets had hit the beast in the legs only. And so, it could not have been gunfire that killed it, although the sudden injuries would have impelled the beast to rush out of its lair. What then had killed this dangerous animal? That was the question. On closer examination we found a massive crack in its skull - the result of the thundering blow that I had administered with my pole. I was congratulated by the hunters. The pole had served us better than bullets!

Though hunting has fallen into disrepute, it had its value, not just for the skills involved in tracking and the capture, or as a once vital means of survival, but as a mental balm. There are many activities recommended for people who suffer from mental fatigue, and I think that hunting in the old days was one of the best. There is no doubt that the drama of the hunt, the concentration required to focus on signs of animals in the environment; and the need to run very fast, all act to sharpen the mind. No-one on a hunt in the wilderness thinks about anything but the hunt!

When stories are told of hunting in Zanzibar, it is usually the wild boar tales which are the most exciting. Hunting wild boar is physically very demanding as it requires the hunter to run fast for extended periods chasing the speeding boar on the run. It was also necessary to protect Zanzibar's agricultural industry by culling wild boar. All over the Island, the farmers' greatest complaint was that wild boars were devouring their crops. When these fierce and rather ugly animals invade a farm, they destroy the fields and wreak havoc in every direction.

Since boars were considered to be a widespread menace, an organization was created to support and regulate wild boar hunting on the Island. The system worked as follows: an acknowledged hunting leader receives a letter from a village chief asking for hunters to come to his district and tackle the boar threat. The leader fixes a date and tells hunters in different parts of the Island where to meet, informing local villagers of the arrangements. The villagers must be involved as it is their obligation to show their appreciation for a job well done by providing food for the hunters when they return to the village at the end of the hunt.

It happened that I had some good friends who went boar hunting almost every weekend. They were a long time in asking me to join them, and, when they finally invited me, I was thrilled. There was a lot to learn. I found that most boar hunters carry spears and very few use guns. Spears are preferable because of the risk of accidentally shooting fellow hunters when surrounding a boar in the bush. Cartridges or bullets can cross the diameter of the encirclement to hit hunters on the other side, whereas spears cannot.

At ten o'clock on the day of the hunt we assembled at a place twenty miles from town. All the hunters were dressed in suitable attire for bushwhacking and running with dogs, as is essential in the heat of the hunt. As soon as the dogs catch scent of a boar, they rush along its trail, barking furiously, while their masters run behind, holding spears ready to hurl at the target.

The most experienced hunters enter the bush first and are quickly followed by the others. When cornered, boars are likely to attack savagely, causing severe wounds to the hunters and their dogs. A hunter usually brings along a needle and thread to sew up his dog's stomach in case of injury. In this particular hunt, the boar had no chance to attack as he was tracked down and speared to death - to the delight of the dogs whose immediate reward was fresh meat. They set upon the fallen beast in a yelping pack, tearing at the raw flesh and gulping it down savagely.

Since I was new to boar hunting, I could be only a spectator. The hunters were divided in groups for the chase, each man running in his own group. Every so often, my group suddenly changed direction, and I couldn't understand why. I soon found out that the hunters in one group must be alert and keep their ears open to pick up signals from other groups which might be first to spot prey.

When a hunter sees a boar, he shouts in a very high-pitched voice, giving only minimal directions like, "north-east!" - and nothing more. The other groups pick up the cry and head in the direction indicated to track down the beast. As I ran with the hunters, I concentrated on discerning the cry, but, no matter how hard I listened, I never heard it. Undoubtedly it takes experience to distinguish the sound of a distant cry in the wilderness.

Boar hunting can be extremely gruelling. One time shortly after the group changed direction, we had to climb a hillock covered with thick brush. I found it tough going, but made it through. When we reached the top, my hands were bleeding. In the rough scramble uphill through the underbrush, my trousers had been ripped away from my knees and they were bleeding too. However, stopping was out of the question; there was a sense of excitement in the air and we had to keep running to catch up with the lead group far ahead. They had made a kill, much to the satisfaction of the dogs. Their high-pitched yelping reverberated in the hills, breaking the silence of the wilderness.

Other groups were also victorious that day - it was reported that no less than ten wild boar had been killed. The villagers were ecstatic. Around the fire that night we talked excitedly about all the details of each kill - who threw the first spear and how the boar died. In the case of our group, the boar ran into the bush and led us in one direction before striking off into another. But the dogs tracking the scent eventually discovered the real route the boar took. We were still extremely anxious because we knew that the delay in finding his new track could give the boar time to escape.

As luck would have it, in the end, the prey was ours. By then we were scraped, bruised, exhausted, and soaked with sweat. The villagers had already prepared water for ablution and mats for prayer. After these calming rituals, we were ready to enjoy the wonderful feast they had prepared for us.

The simple, primal life of the hunt has an elemental appeal, taking us back not only centuries, but millennia - to times when hunting was the only means that human beings had of survival. After the danger and extreme exertion of the hunt, there are few feelings on this earth that can compare with the sheer satisfaction of eating the fresh kill in peace and camaraderie around an open fire.

Chapter 11
A passion for travel

Over the past eight decades, I have had the incomparable good fortune of travelling to many countries in Africa, Europe, North America, the Far East, and the Arab World. There are hundreds of stories to tell, but I shall relate only those that elucidate the main theme of these memoirs – the course of my life before and after the shattering revolution in Zanzibar in 1964.

Just as I was drawn to the excitement of the hunt, I could not resist the lure of travelling. For me, travel was not only a continuation of my education – it was pure adventure. The enticement of travel was present in my consciousness as a young boy – and, with the first exposure, it grew into a passion that only increased with time.

Something inside me came alive when I began studying geography and history. I had a passion to experience the places I had only read about. My travels abroad began in Africa, that vast land mass first known to the outer world as 'The Dark Continent'. My experience of Africa was anything but dark!

Headed for Uganda in the heart of Africa, Samira and I journeyed by train to Nairobi and on to Kampala, the capital. Standing on the platform waiting to receive us was my great friend, Prince Badru Kakungulu Wasajja, whom I had met years earlier through my old friend Hamed Suleiman Al Busaidi of Mombasa. The Prince, an impressive personage, was debonair and had a distinguished old-world charm. He took us to a well-appointed bungalow that he had specially reserved for us. First thing the next morning, the Prince came to see Samira and me, graciously asking whether we had slept well. As a matter of fact, we had slept soundly and had just been served an excellent breakfast.

I should pause to say that Prince Badru Kakungulu Wasajja was a significant political figure in twentieth-century Uganda. His most important achievement was to establish an education system in Uganda that produced a new Muslim elite able to integrate the ideals of Western education with the teachings of Islam. On the political front, the Prince was a diplomatic leader with exceptional negotiation skills. During the divisive era of the Idi Amin regime, Prince Badru argued relentlessly for, and won, an honourable outcome for Muslims, thus averting a holocaust.*

Prince Badru took us on tour of Kampala, followed by a visit to the burial ground of his ancestors in the royal cemetery, an area covered by a large, round shed. This was where all members of the Ugandan royal family and important dignitaries were buried. I was amazed to see women actually living by the graveside. They were various wives and concubines of former kings and princes who had died. It seems that the widows chose to spend the remainder of their lives at the graveside of their loved ones out of respect and undying love. The practice seemed like a less severe form of the 'suttee' practised by some widows in India, who choose, or perhaps are coerced, to climb onto the funeral pyre and succumb to the flames, burning alive with the bodies of their dead husbands.

Prince Badru next showed us his partially finished Islamic school which was already in use. As Prince Badru was an ardent Muslim, the curriculum emphasized the teachings of Islam. Trained in Cairo, the Ugandan teachers spoke Arabic fluently and had excellent grammar. They understood the Holy Qu'ran thoroughly and taught it with full confidence. The Prince gave valuable land to the school and invested

* Kasoki, A, *The Life of Prince Badru Kakungulu Wasajj - The Development of a Forward Looking Muslim Community in Uganda 1907-1991,* Michigan State University Press, East Lansing, 2005.

considerable funds in continuously expanding the facilities and eventually adding secondary studies. This represented a significant achievement for Islamic education in Uganda. The Prince was a man who made history.

One evening, Prince Badru took us to the Palace to meet his cousin, King Kabaka. The Monarch welcomed us in a most gracious fashion, and, conversing in a relaxed fashion, kept us in his company for quite some time. King Kabaka was extremely polite, with a gracious regal presence and wonderful manners - an excellent host. I remember every detail of our meeting with this noble personage.

When Prince Badru came to Zanzibar, he always stayed with me and sometimes brought friends. Hospitality is of utmost importance to me as it is ingrained in my cultural background and is a central component of my own personal philosophy of life. I knew that Ugandans were very fond of a certain dish made by boiling green bananas and red meat. We have a similar and very delicious dish in Zanzibar, but we cook the unripe bananas with meat, chicken or fish in coconut juice and herbs. However, I was concerned to make my guests feel at home in our country, and so I prepared a special authentic dish from our local cuisine that I knew would be a different experience for them.

The result was not what I expected. Although Prince Badru was widely travelled and had eclectic tastes, I could tell that his friends did not like the unusual Zanzibari fare, but they would not admit this. I then decided to try the Ugandan green banana and meat dish, but I cooked it the Zanzibari way in coconut juice and herbs. Suddenly my guests were relaxed and happy. After that, I always ensured that there were cooked bananas on the table and I found other things that they enjoyed - and then I too was happy.

Our relations with the Ugandans grew and deepened over time. King Kabaka's interest in Zanzibar steadily increased, and he was keen to pay us a visit. When King Kabaka was in Mombasa for a football cup, he sent a message to Sultan Khalifa bin Haroub saying that he would like to visit Zanzibar. A few days later, the King and his retinue were welcomed with royal fanfare. King Kabaka stayed at the Aga Khan's guest house and each night I had the pleasure of accompanying him to the Palace for dinner.

One evening, the King said that he was very much impressed with his eminent host, Sultan Khalifa, and that, although their ages differed - the Sultan being much older - it seemed to the King that the Sultan was a suitable companion as he was young at heart. King Kabaka had not expected to find such compatibility in a fellow monarch. The Sultan was well-versed in world affairs and the two Rulers took pleasure in conversing on a wide range of topics. The King asked if he could leave his youngest son with Her Highness, Sayyida Nunuu, to learn Arab manners. Her Highness was very pleased to be entrusted with the delightful little Prince who was just eight years old.

But time marches on; both the King and the Sultan are long gone. Moreover, I am sorry to say that my friend, Prince Badru, passed away several years ago. I preserved the last letter that the Prince sent to me, in which, sadly, he said that he had grown old and feeble. May God rest his soul peacefully in Heaven. I do hope that Prince Badru's school still exists and is doing as well as His Highness would have wished.

I took advantage of the opportunity to explore the more immediate environment on the Kenyan coastline and various islands further out in the Indian Ocean. One of the first places I visited was Bagamoyo, an historical eighteenth-century town on the coast of Tanganyika some seventy-five kilometres north of Dar es Salaam, on the edge of the sea, close to Zanzibar. When it was the capital of German East Africa in the late nineteenth century, Dar es Salaam was the most important trading entrepôt in the area. Two hundred years ago, the town was a vibrant place with a large cosmopolitan population. Business was very good. The harbour at Bagamoyo was easily accessible even for small dhows and fishing boats from Zanzibar. When the winds were favourable, the journey to or from Zanzibar took six to seven hours. This relatively short distance tempted us to plan a sailing trip to Zanzibar. We had a friend in Bagamoyo by the name of Mr Shardel Al Baluchi, who was one of the many residents whose ancestors had lived in the town for more than a century.

Shardel introduced us to the Captain of a small boat, known in Swahili as a *'buti'*. The Captain's nickname was Kijogoo, which means a small cock. Kijogoo told us that, more than thrice a week, he sailed to Zanzibar with a cargo that included quantities of flowers to sell. The flowers were beautifully arranged bouquets of roses with jasmine that filled the boat with an exquisite aroma. Tied on broad green leaves, the jasmine and rose bouquets, called '*kikuba*' in Swahili, were in great demand, especially among the poor who could not afford western perfume.

In addition to the cargo, Kijogoo said he carried a few passengers. After an informal interview we were satisfied that the Captain was an experienced sailor and that it would be safe to sail with him. And so, when our holidays were approaching, we phoned our friend in Bagamoyo to arrange for the boat trip to Zanzibar. When we boarded, we were surprised to find a woman and three men on the dhow. The Captain had mentioned that he carried passengers, but we somehow thought we would be the only ones.

The woman sat in the stern where we were supposed to sit. The stern was about three feet square and the Captain also had to sit in this space to control the rudder. He suggested to the lady that she find another place, but she refused, and so we had to squeeze in between. Because of the strict gender separation codes in our culture, we found the situation both embarrassing and worrying – so much so that, although it was dark and getting late, we could hardly fall asleep.

The three men were from the interior and had never sailed before. They were made to sit in the middle of the boat around a bucket. We knew what was going to happen… and sure enough, once the boat started moving, they became seasick.

At about 10:00 pm, as we approached the small island of Bawe, Captain Kijogoo threw the anchor. We asked him why we had to stay there and for what length of time. Kijogoo authoritatively informed us that the wind was not strong enough for the vessel to continue, and that we had to wait at anchor until dawn when the wind would rise again and we could sail on to Zanzibar.

The Captain suggested that we take a nap, but as this was impossible, we watched the hours slowly drift into the increasing darkness. True to his word, at 5:00 o'clock in the morning, the wind started blowing. Pulling up anchor, we set sail, heading straight for the port in the Malindi district of Stone Town. Thrilled at last to be home again, we forgot all that we had endured during the long night at sea.

In the evening at our club we had to answer endless questions about Dar es Salaam and our trip across the channel. Again, a good night's sleep evaded us, as we had engagements all day long and into the small hours of the morning. After three days of olympic socialising we were exhausted, but made it to the port at the appointed time on the morning scheduled for the return journey. How very relieved and fortunate we felt when we saw Captain Kijogoo waiting for us with the boat ready to sail and no other passengers onboard.

Next, we were pleasantly surprised to have crates of oranges that could be used as seats. This basic amenity seemed like luxury in comparison with the privations of the outward journey. No sooner had we started to move than we fell asleep, waking as we passed Bawe Island. As the boat approached the Island, birds flew overhead as if to say hello again. We drifted back to sleep. At about 5:00 o'clock in the afternoon, the Captain woke us up. When I asked him how much further we had to go. He smiled and said we were already in Bagamoyo.

Heartily thanking him for the comparatively pleasant trip, we told our Captain that Kijogoo, the Cock, had done very well. He smiled broadly. The modest Captain charged us very little and we added a generous tip. It had been a memorable experience to sail over the ocean for hours and hear nothing but the soft whistle of the wind on the sail and the rhythmic sound of the waves breaking on the bow.

I was anxious to venture further afield, and responded to an inspiring advertisement for a tour on a French sailing boat departing Dar es Salaam for Madagascar, the largest island in East Africa. In fact Madagascar was regarded locally as a small continent. The boat would stop at three ports in Madagascar before reaching Mauritius. At the time, these interesting small countries were under French administration.

I phoned my long-time friend, our Oxford oarsman, Said bin Saif bin Salim Al Busaidi who was then in Mombasa, asking him to join me on the tour. As it was short notice, Said Saif had to scramble and catch a plane to Dar es Salaam. In the rush, Said Saif forgot to apply for a visa from the French Consulate in Kenya. We paid for the tour at the agency and collected our tickets and vouchers. No one asked us about our visas, although I had mine, and I thought Said Saif had his too.

We sailed in the evening, first passing the bright lights of the Comoros Islands against the starlit blackness of the night sky at sea. There were many people from the Comoros living in East Africa as there was a lively trade between Zanzibar and the Comoros archipelago, although confined to seasons when the sea was not too rough.

Our first port of call in Madagascar was the main gateway to the country, Tamatave, a French colonial town overlooking a broad sandy harbour on the eastern coast. We were taken on tour through the palm-lined streets of the old town and shown the Jewish quarter where the houses were built unusually close together. This arrangement allowed residents to visit each other without having to travel any distance or spend money. It also facilitated private meetings of the community. It seems that everywhere Jews settle, they live in close quarters, as I noticed the same preference for packed housing with Jewish communities in Austria, Libya and Tunisia.

While in Tamatave we were advised to see the Immigration Officer before we boarded a train to the capital, Antananarivo, ninety miles inland. At first, the Immigration Officer would not allow my visa-less friend to go to Antananarivo. Finally, after long arguments and pleading, Said Saif was granted a visa. Feeling triumphant, we boarded the train for a wonderful scenic journey into the heart of Madagascar. Through the unusually large glass windows of the moving train, we watched verdant fields, beautiful mountains and splendid valleys roll by.

Arriving that evening in Antananarivo, an old city perched on a mountain cliff, we had dinner and sat on the verandah of our hotel in the heights, enjoying the lovely weather and the lights on the terraces below. We heard sweet, soft music and wondered where it came from. Scanning the terrain, we spotted a house on the lower terrace with an open window through which we saw a young couple dancing. It was a romantic image that stayed in my mind and seemed to express my warm feelings for Antananarivo. My attachment and interest increased when I discovered that Antananarivo was named 'The City of the Thousand' because, when it was established by a tribal King named Andrianjaka in the early seventeenth century, a thousand soldiers were assigned to guard it.

The next morning a tray of coffee and a piece of bread with butter was brought to each of us. We thought it was a light, early morning wake-up offering. When we went downstairs and asked the receptionist for breakfast, we saw that he was perplexed. Said Saif and I soon understood that the meager repast we had in bed that morning was meant to be breakfast.

After a real breakfast of tea, eggs and toast in town, we went about looking at shops. Eventually we came upon a square with people selling beautiful flowers. There were also handicrafts and paintings of local scenery and birds with gorgeous colours. All the exhibits had been handmade by students from the School of Art. I wanted very much to visit the school, but, unfortunately it was closed for the holidays.

I was greatly impressed with the range and quality of goods on sale, and it struck me that we should try to improve our handicrafts in Zanzibar. I realized that this would take considerable effort to organize, as Zanzibar's craftspeople lived in different parts of the Island, sometimes great distances apart. Although there was an official in charge of handicrafts in Zanzibar, he was an old man. He did try his best to bring the craftspeople together to discuss ways of improving their products for the tourist trade, but to little avail. A souvenir shop was opened; however, at that time, there were very few tourists coming to Zanzibar.

On my return to Zanzibar, I wrote a report to the Government about the art and crafts school in Antananarivo. The school had been established by a Paris-based organization called South of the Sahara, and I suggested that we seek help from this organization regarding what range of quality goods we might produce and the possibility of eventually establishing our own school of art.

I felt the need was urgent because most of our craftspeople were elderly and it was important that their skills be passed on to the younger generation. The Government of Zanzibar accepted my report and contacted the French Government. The South of the Sahara Art School sent an official who was posted to work under me, instead of under the old man in charge of the Handicraft Office. Not unpredictably, this enraged the old man and his supporters.

The French official tried his best to persuade the craftspeople, especially the silversmiths, to improve their work in the hope of having products that could be exported to Europe and the USA. However, our deliberations did not go well because of resistance whipped up behind the scenes by the old man. The result was that the French official had to wind up his work and leave the country. This was a great pity, for Zanzibar's traditional handicrafts have by now almost disappeared. Instead, shops with mass-produced souvenirs from the mainland cater to the many tourists who currently visit Zanzibar - and these shops do a very good business.

Among the many interesting historical monuments we saw in Madagascar was the palace of the famous 19th Century Queen, Ranavolana, which had been converted into a museum. Inside, was a full scale painting of Queen Ranavolana, a very beautiful woman. I read that Sayyid Said the Great had proposed marriage to her in 1833 in a bid to extend his influence by a dynastic marriage.* After consultation with her Ministers, Queen Ranavolana declined the proposal. It was said that all the Ministers but one advised that this was a personal matter best left to the Queen herself. It was perhaps the Grand Vizier, the chief minister

* Sir Donald Hawley, *Oman,* Stacey International, London 1995, p. 61

of state appointed by France in colonial times, who persuaded Queen Ranavolana of Madagascar that marriage to a monarch from another country might complicate her rule.

Leaving the green isle of Madagascar we stopped briefly at Reunion Island, before journeying on to Mauritius, a beautiful, well-populated island, which unfortunately we had little time to see - something I still regret. It seems that, with travel in the modern era, there is seldom enough time. The consolation is that we can always go back to the places that we did not have time to explore fully; however, the reality is that we seldom do.

But I journeyed more than once to the not far-distant island of Lamu, now a prestigious, up-market destination, although in my day, it was an undeveloped old trading post with a small rural population and transport only by donkey. On my first trip to Lamu, I was taken to see the beautiful doors which had been carved with calligraphic poetry by the famous Lamu poet, Kijuma.

Traditionally, the people of Lamu were cosmopolitan and many were multilingual as a result of frequent contact with traders from Asia, Europe and Arabia. In the past, the main international traders who sailed the seas to Lamu were Chinese, Iraqis and Iranians, but many local dhows from Zanzibar and the neighbouring African coast also came to trade.

The seafarers and skilled craftsmen of Lamu built their own dhows. I once stood watching a dhow under construction and commented that, if the dhow were mine, I would name it 'Munira'. The news reached the owner; and, surprisingly, he gave the dhow that very name. The Islanders were also famous for their beautifully painted stools and chairs of many colours. The pigments came from the craftsmen's extensive knowledge of plants and roots. Many of these brightly coloured stools and chairs have survived the test of time and are found in up-market homes and antique shops today.

When Sultan Hamoud bin Mohammed (1896-1902) visited Lamu, he found the people delightful and cultured. As Sayyid Hamoud was the first Sultan to visit the Island, he was given a joyous welcome with sincere displays of love and loyalty. The people of Lamu entertained their Monarch with splendid dances, exciting theatrical performances and dramatic poetry recitals.

Naturally, Sultan Hamoud was quite touched and very impressed. He noted that many of the young ladies of the Island were pale-skinned beauties and decided to find a wife among them for his son, Sayyid Ali bin Hamoud (1902-1911). My aunt, Khadija Suleiman bin Hamed Al Busaidi, was the one who was chosen!

Sayyid Ali proposed to Aunt Khadija who was brought to Zanzibar for a royal wedding. However, the marriage did not turn out well, as Sayyid Ali bin Hamoud and Sayyida Khadija spoke different languages and found it difficult to learn from each other and communicate. For this and perhaps other reasons, happiness eluded them. They eventually divorced, and my aunt returned to her home in Lamu.

Over the years, I was told many tales about the humourous and eccentric people of Lamu. I remember one story in particular. The Lamu people were known for their love of sweet things. Dhows would come regularly from Lamu to Zanzibar to purchase cargos of delicious sweet dates. Once, when a fully laden dhow was sailing back to Lamu, it was caught in a fierce storm with strong winds and enormous waves. The old wooden craft was tossed about in the wind and waves. Water came rushing in from all sides. The sailors fought a desperate battle against the raging storm, but still there was a very real danger of the dhow sinking. As a last resort, the Captain ordered the crew to drop anchor and throw the cargo overboard to reduce the weight of the vessel.

By the next morning the storm had subsided and the Captain gave orders to set sail and head for home. But the crew implored the Captain to wait while they dove down to retrieve the cargo of fine dates from the bottom of the sea. The sailors could not bear to lose their precious cargo! The Captain reluctantly agreed and the whole crew watched as one enthusiastic sailor dove into the water and quickly disappeared from view. Everyone waited for the sailor to surface with a sack of the coveted dates. But the smooth surface of sea remained silent and undisturbed, except for the odd fish that jumped. There was no sign of the sailor.

What had happened to him? "He must be eating the dates!" cried the crew. A second sailor was dispatched to the depths to search for the first sailor and the valuable missing cargo. Again everyone waited.

The second sailor did not return. What became of him? The crew believed the two sailors were down on the ocean bed eating the dates together! They decided to send a third sailor down. The third sailor was admittedly apprehensive about the mission, but the crew told him he must retrieve the dates before the other two ate the entire cargo!

The third sailor dove beneath the eerily calm surface of the deep blue sea. Everyone waited, scanning the waters. Minutes passed. The third sailor did not return. Finally, not wanting to lose any more crew members, the Captain ordered the dhow to set sail and resume the journey back to Lamu – minus three sailors and the delicious dates.

Lamu is part of our family history, as my great-grandfather had served as the Wali of Lamu and Mogadishu. On my first visit to Lamu, my grandmother suggested I pay a visit to an old friend who lived on the seafront on Ustamui Road. The houses in that area were all extremely close to one another, creating a latticework of slender shaded alleyways that meandered though the old neighbourhood.

When I arrived at my old friend's house and glanced through a window by the door, a curious sight met my eyes – a long assemblage of colour and shape that seemed at first to be a Chinese dragon! I was amazed and could not make sense of the extraordinary sight. It turned out to be an elaborate shroud for ladies who wished to go out during daylight hours.

One maid stood in front of the lady, holding up two crossed sticks, and another maid stood at the rear in the same fashion. A long strip of brightly patterned cloth was strung between the two sets of sticks. Ensuring that she would not be seen by strangers, the lady was securely positioned in the middle as the trio walked along inside the shrouded canopy, like a human centipede.

Lamu Islanders love music and are always quick to sing about any event. They are masters of improvisation, making up wonderfully creative and often humorous lyrics as they go along. Someone would start singing, and almost immediately, from somewhere in the distance, a rejoinder would ring out, and then everyone would be filling the air with song. One famous Lamu song goes like this: "*We went to the seashore together. Nobody saw us there, except the silver stars above, who were our silent witnesses.*"

Music always creates a joyous atmosphere, lifting both the heart and the spirit. I was once told a story which illustrates the Islanders' love of music. The story goes back to the days when dhows from the Gulf region came to Lamu. Whenever a dhow in the Gulf was scheduled to sail, a musician would be employed. He would be considered an important member of the crew, as his music would keep everyone entertained during long voyages. When a commercial dhow from the Gulf arrived in Lamu, the merchant and his men would rent a house where they would stay while the cargo was unloaded and until all business transactions were completed. Usually the merchant would throw a party for the crew, and everyone in town could hear the melodic sound of the oud above the exuberant singing, clapping and tabla drumming.

On one such occasion, there was a sudden knock at the door of a house where a Gulf merchant's party was in progress. One of the crew opened the door a crack and saw, standing there, a group of smiling women who could not resist the call of music. But he closed the door in their faces and shouted, "*This is a private party for men only*". In defiance of the usual gender barrier, the Lamu women replied, "*You cannot have a party without us. You must let us come and join in, otherwise we will break down the door*" ! And so, the door was opened wide, and the women rushed in, singing and clapping!

The people of Lamu once made their living by cutting down mangrove trees and stripping the branches to make poles which they would sell to merchants from the Arabian Gulf. The poles were stained, or in special cases painted in decorative geometric patterns, and used along with palm frond matting and mud to make attractive ceilings for houses in the Gulf.

Lamu was also famous for its religious scholars. The central importance of religion was such that some people made their lives in mosques. One eccentric Muslim who lived in a mosque insisted that he wanted to die without ever seeing a Christian. This was an extremely difficult challenge, as there was no shortage of expatriates and visitors in town. Indeed, the District Commissioner or 'DC' was British - and most definitely a Christian. As he did not want to encounter or offend the DC, this devout Muslim had to use obscure routes whenever he went to and from the mosque.

There was a sort of university in Lamu which was known as Small Azhar University in an allusion to the ancient and well-renowned university of that name in Cairo. It happened that an old religious scholar at Small Azhar University decided to translate the entire Holy Qu'ran from Arabic into Swahili. However, there was some resistance to this idea because of the possibility of misinterpretation. After spending many years on this laborious and exacting task, the old scholar became increasingly aware of the dangers of interpretation and began to fear that he might be vulnerable to serious criticism.

One day the scholar's growing fear overcame good judgment and he impulsively wrapped the translation in a cloth and buried it in the ground, never to be seen again! And so, this first, and no doubt invaluable, translation was lost forever. Those who objected to the translation were not thinking of the great good it would do in spreading Islam to the vast Swahili-speaking population of the region. Sometime later, Sheikh Abdulla Saleh Al Farsi and others openly took on this important task.

As the Island economy declined, and the Government no longer allowed mangroves to be cut down, many people were forced to leave Lamu in search of work. After the discovery of oil, Arabs had become wealthy in their original lands and no longer used mangrove poles in the construction of ceilings. Consequently, the people of Lamu lost a major source of income, and, for this and other reasons, gradually became very poor.

There is a story that expresses the essential pathos of this situation. Once, an Islander who had left Lamu to make his fortune came back to the Island to choose a bride. Former Lamu people and friends came from Kenya, Tanganyika and Zanzibar to celebrate the wedding. When the extravagant festivities were over, everyone gathered at the port to say goodbye to the wedding guests from abroad. A lady from Lamu stood up and sang a song for the passengers who would soon depart on dhows and ferries. The lyrics went something like this:

"*We welcomed you home and were delighted that you came back. Now it is so hard to see our people leave again.* Maskini Lamu Kwa Sikuzake - *Poor Lamu! We grieve and remember the heyday. Now we are degraded, suffering from loss and poverty.*"

Many people wept at the beautiful, heartfelt words. In Zanzibar, to this day, these words are still spoken: "*Masikini Unguja Kwa Sikuzake.*" Unguja is an old name for Zanzibar, and thus, in the same way as Lamu once was grieved, so is Zanzibar.

The Arab and Islamic world was naturally a focus for my travels. I once went by taxi from Lebanon to Damascus. It was an unforgettable journey. I remember the magnificence of the scenery - green fields spreading to the horizon and sparkling streams running alongside the road. I wanted to ask the driver to stop so that we could camp in the beautiful countryside.

We arrived at the Syrian border early in the morning. After our passports were checked, we journeyed on to Damascus. I stayed in a new hotel not far from a thriving vegetable market with ripe produce artistically displayed in an array of bright colours. For lunch, I went to a nearby restaurant where a trickling stream was channelled through the dining area. Tempting dishes were placed in a glass cabinet so that patrons could examine the fare and make a selection. A few of the dishes on the menu were known to me because they were popular in Zanzibar. To this day, I remember how delicious that lunch was.

The hamam, or Roman-style public steam bath, the precursor of the modern spa, is an important institution in Damascus. I went to a popular hamam with a guide who explained each and every area of the intricate building. There were different places for specialized treatment to relieve specific complaints such as rheumatism or arthritis.

It is both interesting and a source of comfort to note the similarities among the cultures of the Arab and Islamic world. I found myself remembering the hamam in Zanzibar built by the Iranians who accompanied Shazadeh, the Iranian Princess who married Sayyid Said the Great. There was a feeling of luxury as all the rooms in our Persian-Zanzibari hamam were lined with marble. The design included rectangular spaces for steam treatment to be followed by a massage.

One of my most interesting trips was to Turkey. I had read about Turkey's involvement in the First World War when that country was a German ally, and how eventually the war extended to Turkish soil. As is well-known, there was a disastrous battle fought between the British and the Turkish at the Dardanelles, the sea passage to the Black Sea controlled by Turkey. One of the books I read, '*The Triangle*', explained the importance of this crucial waterway and the strategies used in the Battle of the Dardanelles.

I stayed in a hotel overlooking the Dardanelles where I liked to sit on the verandah watching the ships as they navigated through the traffic in the narrow passage. Ships of all kinds passed each other every few minutes. Sometimes I would visualize the momentous events of World War I and the toll it took on both sides. It was almost as if history came alive.

On a tour of Istanbul I admired the iconic Blue Mosque with its elegant spires and multiple-dome architecture. Built in the early seventeenth century (1606-1616) during the reign of Sultan Ahmed I, the mosque still officially bears his name, but almost everyone calls it 'the Blue Mosque' - not because it is coloured blue, but because of the beautiful blue tiles on the interior.

This world-famous mosque is stunningly beautiful - far more so than in the pictures I had seen, and even than I had imagined. Like everyone,

I was impressed with the huge mosaics with awe-inspiring religious figures set in gold. I noticed a special raised platform where the Kings of Turkey prayed on Friday mornings amid the awe-inspiring splendour of this immense mosque. There is so much beauty in the art of the Islamic world!

We saw all the marvels of this ancient city once known as Constantinople. I was fascinated by the sophisticated underground water storage system used particularly during periods of water shortage. It was a marvel of engineering. The covered bazaar of Istanbul - the fifteenth-century 'Grand Bazaar' - is one of Istanbul's most popular attractions. This famous old bazaar with its rich array of goods in some 4,000 shops is housed in a vast building, artistically constructed with grand arches and beautifully carved pillars.

A monument of great historical significance is the old Ottoman Palace, Topkapi, which for four centuries (1465-1856) was the royal headquarters of the longest-standing empire in world history (*circa* 1299-1923). It was wonderful to experience the magnificent architecture and luxurious contents of Topkapi Palace, including handsome turbans studded with emeralds and diamonds - and to have some understanding of the grandeur of the Ottoman Sultans. We saw how the Ottoman Sultans lived and were served - including the kitchens, the splendid crockery and finely made cutlery that was in use until the early twentieth century.

I am not trying to be a modern day Ibn Battuta* and relate everything I came across in my travels around the world - only some of the most interesting journeys and those that are directly relevant to these memoirs and to my thoughts on life as it unfolds – whether in Thailand, Japan the USA or Canada.

*Ibn Battuta (Hajji Abu Abdullah Muhammad Ibn Battuta, *circa* 1369-1404) was a Moroccan traveller and Islamic scholar who wrote a detailed account of his observations during extensive travels in Africa, the Middle East and Asia over a period of thirty years.

I'll never forget an incident that occurred while I was in a hotel in Thailand. When I went to the manager for assistance with a problem in my room, he asked me whether I was an Arab. I replied, "Yes, I am". The manager then told me that there were some Israelis staying in the hotel. Apparently the Israelis had come to him and rather worriedly told him there was an Arab staying in the hotel. They wanted it on record that if anything were to happen to them, I would be held responsible! I told the manager I was a peaceful man and that I had not come to harm anyone…

I have been lucky enough to travel to the United States of America three times. My son Ahmed was studying at St Louis College University and he invited me to attend his graduation. This very happy occasion was the second time I had attended one my children's graduations. The first was Rawya's august graduation ceremony at the University of Oxford in 1988. Steeped in history going back to antiquity, the ceremony was incredibly impressive as all the proceedings were spoken in Latin!

Japan was one of the most fascinating countries I have visited and I shall never forget the tour we took of the city of Hiroshima where the atomic bomb was dropped on the 6th of August 1945 to end World War II. It was a devastating, mind-shattering scene. Everything standing had been utterly destroyed. I was moved to the core of my being and felt incredibly sad. The people of Hiroshima are still suffering the after effects of this horrific tragedy.

It is extremely regrettable, to say the least, that the scientists who developed the atomic bomb did not visualize the irreparable damage it would cause to human beings. The soil of Hiroshima still shows the marks of that unspeakably terrible event. All the resources that are expended today on weapons of mass destruction would be so much better spent on health, education and job creation.

The Japanese have a rich and fascinating culture. I think they are not only intellectually clever, but wise. They, and only they, have experienced the horror and dreadful tragedy of atomic warfare. Commendably, the Japanese response was an eternal commitment to peace.

I have also seen some of the great wonders of nature. Among these is Niagara Falls on the Canada-US border, which filled me with awe. It was breath-taking in every sense of the word. The sound and sheer force of a vast river plunging down a steep, fifty-two metre cliff is stupendous. The Maid of the Mist, a kind of tug boat with a powerful engine, took tourists close to where the pounding, fast-falling waters hit the surface of the river.

To see such a wondrous phenomenon is truly to marvel at God's creation - why He chose to create a desert with no water where human beings and plants are so thirsty, and at the same time, a phenomenon in which unimaginable volumes of water - some six hundred million cubic feet per minute, pour into an already full river. It is amazing to think that such a quantity of water is more than enough to supply the needs of many lands and create infinite fields of green crops.

This is not a world where we can forever travel; one must always come back to the realities of life. I began this volume with the event that changed my life forever – the Revolution in Zanzibar, and to that we now return.

On a Greek Island

In Spain with family

During my tour of France

In Africa with Samira

Chapter 12
Unseen, the gathering storm

It is a truism that change is the only constant in life. We know this, yet we tend to wrap ourselves in the illusion of small, safe worlds where it seems certain that things will stay the same, or that change is for the better.

After the violence of the Second World War, the 1950's and early 1960's seemed a placid period, a time for family life and a secure career. But, in Zanzibar, storm clouds were slowly gathering. At times I sensed this, and stopped to think about the vague but gnawing signs of danger that were accumulating. I even understood many of the elements that eventually spelled disaster, but I did not grasp the full magnitude of the storm that was brewing. And so, for me, as well as for most other Arab Zanzibaris, the magnitude of the gathering storm, Zanzibar's looming Armageddon, was largely unseen.

Politics were at the root of the problem. Zanzibar in the first half of the twentieth century was not an exception among the colonies and protectorates in Africa as far as accelerated political activity and aspirations of independence were concerned, even though Zanzibar and Pemba had a combined population of only about 400,000.

Zanzibar was cosmopolitan, with people of African, Arab and Indian descent living in separate communities. The British governed the Island along ethnic lines. When they decided to promulgate a decree, they had first to assess how the decree would affect the different ethno-cultural constituencies, African, Arab or Indian. They had to consider whether the new decree would suit everyone, or if it might cause upheaval in any one of the three main communities.

127

Often a decree had to be amended many times in order to suit everyone. This was not an easy task. The lack of emphasis on national allegiance for residents of Zanzibar meant that people identified themselves by genetic origin rather than as citizens of the country in which they lived, and, in many cases, had lived for generations. Consequently there was little national cohesion.

However, one of the good things about the operational structure of Zanzibar's British administration was the formation of many committees and boards where the different communities were represented and could give their views. And people who spoke up were definitely not bulldozed. I believe, however, if the British Government had introduced the idea of a Zanzibar nationality, so that everyone would have a sense of identity and national allegiance, it would have strengthened the Government of Zanzibar. One of the peculiarities was that it was possible for a group of Zanzibaris to go to an outside country to lobby for the boycott of competitor's goods from Zanzibar, and then they could come back triumphant and continue their business without interference.

I wonder whether the British public or Government would allow, for instance, a French Member of Parliament to come to Britain to speak at a public meeting in the interest of the Conservative Party, condemning socialism and communism during election time. As far as I know that has never occurred in the United Kingdom, or any other country. Freedom of speech has its limits. Official interference from another country would not be tolerated anywhere. But, shockingly, the British Government allowed it in Zanzibar, in spite of the protests of prominent Zanzibari-Omani officials.

One ethnic community was pitched against another, and that is how the seeds of hatred were planted. Unfortunately, inter-ethnic hatred grew and spread like wild fire.

I believe that if the Government had introduced the idea of nationality earlier, so that people could be identified as Zanzibari nationals, then many problems could have been avoided and the Government would have been strengthened. Citizens and residents would have understood the source of interference in their internal affairs and would have guarded their interests.

In 1914, a British 'Protectorate Council' was created under the nominal presidency of the Sultan. The Council was composed of representatives of the colonial power and the Sultan's Councillors. The duty of the Council was to manage the interior affairs of the country. In 1926, an Executive Council and a Legislative Council were set up, but, surprisingly, Africans were not represented on these Councils until 1945.

After the Second World War, London promoted multi-community policies. Two Africans were appointed as members of the Legislative Council. The Coutts Commission proposed that half of the members of the Legislative Council be elected and called 'non official' by a unique electoral college. This reform was adopted in 1956. During the 1957 election, which was marred by violence, there was a burst of African nationalism.

During the last years before independence, the struggle between the Arabs and the Africans of Zanzibar intensified. Constitutional Commissioner, Sir Hillary Blood, proposed a system based on a Government responsible to a mostly elected Legislative Council. However, the January 1961 election did not yield a clear majority. A new election, once again marred by violence, was organized.

Politics curried by those who may be immature, arrogant or insufficiently knowledgeable can be very dangerous. It surprised me, and I could not bring myself to believe, that the British Government, with all its statesmanship in India and other places, could not visualize the consequences of allowing such freedom of activity - in spite of the protests raised by junior Zanzibari members of the public administration. It was political mismanagement of this kind which would destroy Zanzibar.

The question of the 'haves' and 'have-nots' is a common subject pertaining to conditions all over the world. Zanzibar was no exception. There was a desire for a better standard of living by those who had no productive ambition or any real knowledge of how to better themselves. All over the world, human nature unfolds in the strong trying to dominate the weak. This was characteristic of the economic situation of Zanzibar which divided people into different status groups according to their means of earning a living.

There were smart business people who sat at their desks all day buying and selling. There were affluent farmers who had workers to tend to their clove and coconut orchards as they sat at home enjoying the proceeds from the sale of their crops. And everywhere there were workers of all kinds and small entrepreneurs, such as shopkeepers.

Although part of Zanzibar is made of coral, the Island can feed itself because the land is fertile and the soil is rich in nutrients, and, although there are no major rivers, the Island has abundant sources of fresh water in springs. Ships entering the waters of East Africa often came to Zanzibar to buy fresh sweet water, as it was the best available. Captains were happy to pay a good price for Zanzibar's water as they were aware that the Government took care to ensure that it was clean and pleasant to taste. That is how Zanzibar became prosperous before other countries in East Africa.

Many different peoples came to Zanzibar, mainly from Tanganyika, Kenya, East Asia, the Arabian Gulf and Europe. As the capital, Zanzibar Town developed into a cosmopolitan city, I came across a Kurd family, as well as Egyptian and Chinese families, all of whom were settled in

Zanzibar. The Kurd family, from Northern Iraq, intermarried with local people. There were also Turks. As for Iranians, several large families made their homes in Zanzibar. Most of the Iranian immigrants had come to the Island as clergy for the Shia population.

Omanis had been coming to East Africa for many centuries as traders and as settlers. During the monsoon period, when the north-east winds blew from the Arabian Sea to East Africa, Omani dhows set sail. Many of them carried cargoes for trade in small ports along the eastern coast of Africa in countries such as Somalia where they stopped for supplies and fresh water. Some ships also stopped at Lamu and Mombasa, while others sailed straight to Zanzibar. These ships usually carried a good cargo of Omani dates as well as salted dried fish which were sold over a wide area in East Africa, including Kenya and Tanganyika.

Life in Zanzibar was comparatively easy because produce grew quickly in the fertile soil and frequent rains. In the interior, most residents and farmers grew their daily food in garden plots just behind their houses. They cultivated banana trees and a variety of vegetables. They also kept chickens and goats. Those Omanis who managed to open shops did reasonably well, but most did not earn enough to be affluent, as they had to sell their commodities at a cheap price to suit the pockets of their customers, many of whom were quite poor. I noticed that those Omanis who had shops in the most fertile and highly populated areas were better off because their customers could afford higher prices.

The newcomer had to earn a lot in order to build a successful new life. Some began by taking loans to buy coconuts from local farms to make copra which they would sell in town for a small profit. Others laboured directly on the plantations. They worked hard and quickly assimilated the language. Some took part in political life.

Zanzibar had a Legislative Council with official membership of the Heads of Departments, as well as Ministers and representatives of the main communities - Zanzibaris, Arabs, Indians and others. I have used the name 'Zanzibaris' rather than 'Africans' because I feel the latter is too general a term since it includes many different cultures and peoples.

During the process of political change, parties were formed. Naturally, each party had to create a platform of arguments on issues and causes for which to fight in the election process. Unfortunately, the Afro-Shirazi Party chose to conduct their campaign along ethnic lines; whereas, the opposing party, the Nationalist Party which was comprised of different minority groups, fought for general benefits for the entire country. The Nationalist Party therefore became very popular and won the election.

The National Party campaigned on the slogan, *Zanzibar for Zanzibaris*, while the Afro-Shirazi Party argued for everything African. The Afro-Shirazi doctrine implied that Zanzibar was part of Africa and should therefore open its doors to mainland Africans and their interests. The idea was that the rest, all non-Africans, were foreigners who were blamed for slavery.

The Afro-Shirazi Party leader often admitted that his party was not yet ready to run a government, but he declared that, on winning the election, he would ask the British Government to teach his followers how to govern the country. This meant that British personnel would remain on the Island as long as they were needed. Of course, this declaration was very much welcomed by representatives of the British Government and led them to believe that their friendship was very much needed.

After the Revolution, two or three British officials, a remaining few - since almost all the British had by then left the Island - pleaded with the Afro-Shirazi Party leader, Abeid Karume, when he was elected President of the newly independent Zanzibar, to continue with British assistance. But the President rejected this plea - to the astonishment of the British officials, as they thought that this rejection was contrary to his pre-election promise of retaining the British officials of the former Zanzibar Civil Service after the Revolution. Although the British knew that Karume was an illiterate worker, they allowed themselves to be deceived. It was incredible!

As preparations were made for Zanzibar's independence, the first step was to grant internal independence. The Nationalist Party, as mentioned, won the self-rule election, but created a harsh environment saturated with hatred. I feel this came from inter-ethnic animosity – in other words, racial hatred - fuelled by allusions to slavery, still an extremely sensitive subject and one that was used to advantage in politics.

Aggressive speeches at public meetings continued unabated as the Government chose not to interfere. Apparently the British excused their lack of action on the grounds that it allowed freedom of speech. It was a situation that was bound to foment hatred and aggression. The Opposition Afro-Shirazi party's motto was *Africa for Africans*, while the Nationalist Party was multi-ethnic, recognizing all residents as Zanzibaris.

Many African residents on the mainland as well as the Afro-Shirazi party promulgated the view that Zanzibar was part of the African continent and that Africans from anywhere could enter and leave Zanzibar without passports and even take part in the election. Indeed, the Afro-Shirazi Party brought hundreds of Africans from Tanganyika to register for the election. Of course, since the Nationalist Party and the British Government knew what was going on, there was no way forward except to make arrangements with each appointed party representative to examine the registries and find out whether the voters were residents of Zanzibar. In this process, many were disqualified.

The election registry was based on residency in Zanzibar, not on legal registration as Zanzibaris. In my opinion, this was wrong. Residents should have been sorted into Zanzibaris and non-Zanzibaris. Those who were not Zanzibari should have been given time to apply for official Zanzibari nationality. The next step would have been registration of legal Zanzibaris as voters in the election. If this had been done, it would have been very hard for people to cheat. Instead, hatred and ethnic bias were stirred up in mass party meetings as well as fomented through the Afro-Shirazi newspaper. Nowhere else in the British Empire was this sort of thing allowed. It seemed beyond comprehension that the British stood by and let it happen.

In the Nationalist Party there was a man known widely by the nickname of Babu. Born and bred in Zanzibar, Babu's full name was Abdulrahman Mohammed Babu (1924-1996). A well-educated thinker and analyst, he dreamed of becoming an important political figure. Babu had read widely and noted how communist leaders rose to fame from nothing. This gave Babu dreams of glory and inspired him to become a Communist. He then had a platform to befriend impressionable young people and proselytize.

Babu contacted communist officials in China who were delighted to find an educated and intelligent young man whom they felt could help spread Communism in East Africa and particularly in Zanzibar. They understood the implications of the old saying, "When a flute is played in Zanzibar, Africans in the Lake areas dance". It was well-known that colonialism in East Africa started in Zanzibar.

The Afro-Shirazi Party realized that it too should seek external aid. Following in the footsteps of Babu, representatives of the Afro-Shirazi Party paid a visit to certain officials in communist China arguing that they were the ones who deserved help - not Babu who belonged to an affluent party. It was said that the Chinese then advised Babu to change course and join the Afro-Shirazi Party - and that is just what Babu did.

I knew Babu fairly well. An unhappy person with no means of support, Babu naturally aspired to bring about change for his own benefit. He seemed to be extremely resentful of those who succeeded in life. The Chinese knew how to manipulate Babu - they paid him well. I remember people saying that when Babu opened his wallet in bars and clubs, they could see that he had big bundles of notes. Once Babu went to a bar in Dar es Salaam, and even though the bar was crowded with people, Babu ordered the bartender to give a free round of drinks to everyone. Babu felt very powerful when everyone in the bar stood up to hail him.

One day, I happened to be present when Babu was sitting with some friends, and so, I heard their conversation. Babu said it would be easy to stage a coup in Zanzibar, adding that he could do precisely that. It appears Babu was heavily involved in planning the coup that eventually took place in Zanzibar. Not only that - he had recruited fighters from Tanganyika who crossed the channel in their hundreds in mechanized boats owned by a Jewish European fisherman, as well as in small fishing boats. They were fully armed and prepared for the coup.

It seems that the plot had a broad regional base. Afro-Shirazi President, Abeid Karume (1964-1972) and President Julius Nyerere of Tanganyika (1964-1985) must have discussed the coup together as they plotted the future of Zanzibar. It was said that President Nyerere had informed the British Government that Zanzibar must belong to Tanganyika since Zanzibar was, after all, a small island separated from Tanganyika by only thirty five miles of water. So the British Government knew what was going to happen after the coup.

President Nyerere was in the pocket of the British Government who had a vision of greatness for him. Nyerere was being groomed to become President of an East African Union, but this was rejected by President Jomo Kenyatta of Kenya. Apparently, Nyerere was also under the influence of Chinese communism and greatly admired its achievements. After a visit to China, Nyerere changed his style of dressing to that of the Chinese. Appreciating the Chinese for their hard work, he revived *ujamaa* or 'familyhood', the idea of working together for the benefit of all – a form of collectivism and socialism. He set up thousands of cooperative village units based on the concept of *ujamaa*.

Lecturing all over Tanganiyka on the subject of *ujamaa*, Nyerere even took part in ploughing the land. As he was a good role model, the people of Tanganyika listened to Nyerere and followed him. The British press spoke highly of him. However, when Nyerere started to nationalize foreign properties including those of the British, they were shocked and deeply disappointed.

There is an Arab proverb to the effect that not all the winds that blow are in accord with the wishes of sailing ships. I was surprised that the British Government, with all its experience in the colonies, failed to sense the hidden objectives of African leaders like Abeid Karume and Julius Nyerere, and allowed themselves to be misled. To this day, I can hardly believe what appears to be an astonishing naiveté on the part of the British.

I could see that changes were imminent in Zanzibar. I felt that the Royal Family had lost touch with the people for quite some time. Sayyid Khalifa was then an old man, yet he remained on the throne until he died at about ninety years of age. At one point, I suggested to Sultan Khalifa that his son, Sayyid Abdulla, might embark on a kind of 'meet the people' tour on the Monarch's behalf. Sayyid Khalifa appreciated my suggestion, and, after about a year, arrangements were made for Sayyid Abdulla to visit Pemba with the British Resident. But Sayyid Abdulla did not make the most of this venture, as he was not a natural leader like his father and had no desire to be in the limelight.

When his father died in 1960, HH Sayyid Abdulla acceded to the throne. He was already over fifty years old. Unfortunately, Sultan Abdulla did not really take to his new role as Monarch. He said that the death of his father had affected him immensely. Sultan Abdullah did not seem to have his heart in ruling the nation. Bad health was also a factor in the Sultan's lack of enthusiasm for the throne. He suffered from progressive blood circulation problems as well as diabetes. I talked with the Sultan about his deteriorating health on a number of occasions. It was plain to see that HH Sayyid Abdulla was losing weight and becoming weak. At a certain point, I urged him to seek immediate medical attention.

In short, it was a combination of a declining Sultanate, divisive British politics and African unrest that led to the devastating Revolution of 1964.

With Sir Alfred Hollis and Zanzibar Government Officials
The Author is third from the left, second row

The Author is third from the left, first row

Chapter 13
Revolution

A series of momentous events in Zanzibar in the early 1960s were to have tragic consequences. The British had begun the process of dismantling their empire, and, with the dawn of the New Year in 1961, constituencies were drawn up and democratic elections held in Zanzibar. The result was a tie between the two main parties, the Nationalist and the Afro-Shirazi, necessitating a second election six months later. The final outcome was a coalition government and persistent allegations of electoral fraud. Not surprisingly, the political situation began to deteriorate and the country grew more and more unstable. The end result was civil disorder with scores of people losing their lives in the fray. The Government took a hard line by banning radical opposition parties, but paramilitary groups formed and the police became politicized.

Complete independence from British rule was granted at the end of 1963. While the celebrations may have seemed normal, people were uneasy as underlying conflicts began to break through the fragile surface of everyday activities and the air was charged with tension. Rumours were circulating about the danger posed by the Afro-Shirazi Party. Judging by the strength of the indignation that the Afro-Shirazi Party adherents expressed in their newspaper, they were seriously aggrieved by their failure to win the election. The core party members felt humiliated; it was obvious that they could not accept the new Nationalist Government.

Rumour after rumour gave credence to the suspicion that the Afro-Shirazi party was preparing for an armed rebellion with help from Tanganyika. Nevertheless, the Nationalist Government was wholly unprepared to contend with the armed uprising that had long been brewing and boiled over on the 12th of January, 1964. It took the Rebels only one hour to rout the police force and defeat the so-called

139

Zanzibar army that consisted only of about two hundred inexperienced soldiers who had been hurriedly trained. Both the army and the police force had been infiltrated. Most of the troops and police simply refused to defend the country. Just a few loyal police officers stood up to fight to the end. These men I saw with my own eyes towards midnight on the day of the coup. They told me that they phoned their Commissioner urging him to come to the scene, but he did not.

Many people knew that the situation after Independence was extremely volatile and fraught with danger. The Nationalist Party asked for military assistance from Egypt, but it did not arrive in time. In spite of the unhelpful behaviour of the British during the election, it must be admitted that the British Government did offer to keep a British force in Zanzibar after Independence.

Unfortunately, the new Government declined the offer, expecting, or perhaps only hoping, that the Egyptian forces would arrive soon. They forgot the old proverb, 'A bird in the hand is worth two in the bush.' I felt it was foolish of the new Government to refuse the offer when they had already been warned from different quarters, including by their own people, that insurrection was looming like a black cloud overhead. This was no secret.

Among those who provided prescient advice to leaders of the Nationalist Government was the Secretary General of the United Nations, U Thant. When the new Government officials went to the United Nations to present their credentials, U Thant told them that it was easier to win the election and form a Government than it was to maintain order after Independence.

It seemed to me that our leaders took the words of the Secretary General with hardly as much as a grain of salt. Drunk on pride, they were not thinking seriously about their responsibilities, especially to the people – and soon the cracks began to appear. They made crucial errors in judgment with disastrous consequences. A new government facing a crisis absolutely must have an experienced and effective administration, yet they removed the very people who had the expertise they needed. The officers who knew the people and the areas concerned were no longer in charge. This meant a failure of intelligence. Important information no longer reached the Government and the worst case scenario came into play – a violent revolution.

I remember looking out of my window and seeing Sayyid Jamshid, His Highness the Sultan, being driven away from the Palace in his car. He was alone. The other members of the immediate Royal Family were travelling in a second car. Both cars were bound for the port. No rebels entered Malindi until HH Sultan Jamshid and his family had passed through the area. Safe passage for the Royal family must have been part of the British Government's agreement with the rebels.

The truth was that Mr Smithyman, Advisor to Nationalist Prime Minister, Mohammed Shamte, was in touch with the British High Commissioner who ensured a safe royal departure by car to the harbour, then by boat to Tanganyika. President Nyerere arranged for his ministers to cordially receive the royal émigrés and allowed them to remain in Dar es Salaam until a flight to London could be arranged.

A reluctant witness to history, I watched the melancholy departure of the Monarch and his family, and realizing how profound the consequences would be, I thought of leaving too. But what was uppermost in my mind was the heavy weight of my responsibilities in Zanzibar. I was raised never to shirk duty, especially with respect to family obligations - and my widowed sister, Sayyida Nunuu, who was living alone in Zanzibar, needed me to take care of her.

As mentioned in the opening chapter of this book, on the first day of the Revolution, Mr Abeid Karume was declared President of Zanzibar.

On the second day, he paid a visit to all government departments demanding the keys to all offices. On the third day, a young man, one of the so-called Communist Babu's followers, came to my office, arrested me and took me to the Police Station along with others. From there we were marched off to the Voice of Zanzibar Radio Station where General Okello ordered us to be sent forthwith to prison.

When we arrived at the Stone Town Prison, we had our particulars recorded, after which we were led to a crowded cell block where we found many friends and colleagues. As clear as day, I remember that we were each given a coconut fibre mat to sleep on, and only a cloth cover for warmth. I used my shoes as a pillow. As all the wards were overflowing with former government officials, some of us, including me, had to sleep in the corridor facing a big iron door. This was a blessing in disguise because the door had partial openings which allowed cool air and light to enter the ward.

Early in the morning we would take our mats outside into the sunshine, and then bring them back in again at six o'clock in the evening when the prison guards locked us in. In the meantime each prisoner was enlisted to work all day long at some lowly maintenance job like cleaning the exercise yard.

We were allowed to receive food from our families at lunch time. I think this saved the Government considerable expense, but it was also good for us to be spared the extremely unappetizing prison food known as *dona* which consisted of plain cornmeal cooked in water, like porridge. The only difference was that the cornmeal had a bone in it. To our bitter disappointment, this one joy – home-cooked food – soon came to an end. Someone with power must have complained about prisoners being allowed to live in luxury with home-cooked food delivered each day, instead of having to suffer prison rations.

We were allowed to receive certain visitors. One of those who came to see me and say goodbye was the Private Secretary to the British Resident, Mrs Joyce Lavaratt, a friend whose kindness I shall always remember. Red Cross staff from the United Kingdom came and asked us if we had any messages to give to our families and if we had any particular affairs that required attention.

My daughter, Rayyan, was at Alice Oatley Boarding School in England, and I had to withdraw her because I could no longer meet the expenses. I asked Miss London, one of the Red Cross Officials, to do me the favour of arranging for Rayyan to be taken out of school and driven to the airport. Rayyan was put on a plane bound for Egypt so that she could stay with her maternal grandmother in Cairo until further notice. It was a great relief to hear that Rayyan arrived safely in Cairo. I am tremendously grateful to the Red Cross, and to Miss London in particular, for helping me in a time of need.

After about ninety long days, the President himself came to the prison along with an entourage. All the prisoners were told to stand in line. The President passed by and those who were to be released were told to form a separate line. On the advice of the Presidents' followers, the remaining prisoners were to remain incarcerated. As good fortune would have it, I was among those who were to be released.

As I left the prison and breathed the fresh air of freedom, I realized that Zanzibar had changed forever and my elation evaporated. Thousands of people had been killed during the Revolution. Those who had managed to escape had fled into the interior where they hid in the bush and many died of starvation. It was a dreadful time for the people of Zanzibar.

During the heat of the Revolution, many Omanis who were known as active members of the Nationalist Party were arrested, tortured and executed. As far as I know, one of the first high-profile Arabs to be murdered by the Rebels was Nasser bin Issa Al Ismaily whose son, Issa, was Assistant Private Secretary to the British Resident. Other Arabs were massacred in the streets without mercy. Countless thousands of Arabs lost their lives in the course of a single month.

One evening about a fortnight after we were released, I was returning home accompanied by my little son, Ahmed, when I saw several policemen standing outside the door of my house. One of the policemen told me that I was required to present myself at Malindi Police Station. With a sinking heart, and a brave face for my son, I gave him to his nanny, instructing her to take him to my sister, Sayyida Nunuu who lived nearby.

Almost as soon as I arrived at the police station, I was driven away in a police van, straight back to prison. This time, I was thrown into a dark cell where all sorts of criminals and murderers were kept. It was truly mortifying. I thought for sure that I would be killed at dawn. My entire body grew numb from fear and anxiety. I was extremely concerned about my family. How would they manage without me?

At about one o'clock I heard the sound of police boots approaching. The warden opened the door and put a bucket inside. After about an hour another man was interned. When the door of my cell opened, this man saw only a shadow inside, so he asked who his companion was. I gave my name in reply. In that moment, my new cellmate and I exclaimed in one voice as we realized that we knew each other very well. It was my old friend, Mohammed Masoud Al Riyami. As we found it impossible to sleep on the cement floor, we went on chatting until dawn.

At eight o'clock in the morning the Chief Prison Officer came and all the prisoners who had been rounded up the night before were assembled in the compound. He said he had received urgent orders the day before, from the President, ordering our arrest, but he had not been given any reasons. In the morning he made enquiries and found that we were all completely innocent.

It appeared that someone had misled the President. The authorities realized that there were no charges against me and that my incarceration was totally unjustified. My heart surged when the Commissioner of Police announced that we were to be discharged. He went on to say that we were being released on condition that we did not congregate together.

As had been announced by the President, my Omani colleagues and I were dismissed from the Civil Service. The President called us to his office in the former British Resident's house where we were gravely received and told that Mr Julius Nyerere, the President of Tanganyika, was prepared to give us jobs in Dar es Salaam. Then we dispersed.

The Omani residents of Zanzibar had settled mainly in the countryside or *shamba* where they owned shops. Unlike other ethno-cultural groups that lived in close proximity so that they could easily socialize and trade together, Omanis preferred to live at a distance from each other. And so, when the Revolution took place, Omanis could not easily gather together to defend themselves. Thousands died at the hands of armed groups who hunted them down and killed them in cold blood.

Quite a number of Omanis had licensed guns, but, just before the Revolution, a police official went around the countryside on an official gun check. All guns were collected on the excuse that they needed servicing. Receipts were issued and people were told that, after they had been repaired, the guns could be collected by their owners. This was obviously a subterfuge. When the crisis came, people did not have any guns with which to defend themselves.

There was no mercy for the defenceless; they were simply slaughtered. The revolutionary leaders arranged two camps for rural Arabs who managed to reach Zanzibar Town - one for men and the other for women. The camps were in a very crowded, small area at Raha Leo, close to the Radio Station. It took several weeks before the town was calm and the refugees were allowed to go back to their dwellings in the country. Many

Arabs were afraid to return to their homes, and, when they did, they found nothing in them. Some houses had been burned to the ground.

Shortly after the coup, it was announced on the radio that Marshall Okello, the head of the Revolutionary Guard would drive around the town with his chief comrades. People were to remain in their houses. Next, they were told to go outside and wait along the road to greet Marshall Okello by kneeling down when he passed. Everyone obeyed this order.

It was not easy for Arabs to leave Zanzibar in the aftermath of the Revolution. Many escaped in sailing boats to neighbouring ports where they hoped to find safe passage on a steamboat. Some Omanis were able to fly out, while others waited for monsoon dhows to take them back home or to any port in the Gulf.

Some Arabs managed to get to Mombasa. From there, they tried to stow away on steamboats. In order to avoid detection some hid in the animal pens on board. It must have been dreadful to be cooped up with animals during the long trip to the Gulf. In most cases, the dhows encountered storms and rough seas; consequently, when the passengers disembarked in the Gulf, they were in a bad state.

Those who were destined for Oman were unable to disembark in Muscat for political reasons, and so the dhows took them to Dubai. In one instance, a group of refugees without passports was dumped on the beach at Dubai; and, after several days on the shore in the glare of the sun and without sustenance, one man died. His nickname was Mbwa Koko, which means 'stray dog'.

Before he died, the man was hallucinating. He kept asking when they were going back to Zanzibar. His companions on the beach felt deeply saddened to lose their friend, especially in a country where they hoped they would find refuge. They all experienced severe hardship before finally reaching Oman, the home of their ancestors.

Chapter 14
Fleeing Zanzibar

When I returned to my official residence after being released from prison for the second time, I realized, with a heavy heart, that I no longer had a future in Zanzibar. It was time for me to leave my beloved island.

I was not the first in the family to leave. Samira moved to Dar es Salaam where she had secured a job. As we had divorced in the wake of the Revolution, Samira had taken our youngest child, Ahmed, with her. However, after some time in Tanganyika, Samira felt she and Ahmed were not safe even there. They made a very daring escape, driving through dark, forested areas for most of the night and finally reaching Mombasa early in the morning. They boarded the first flight to Nairobi with a connection to Cairo where they joined Rayyan and Rawya at Samira's parents' house. I remained in Zanzibar with my sister, Sayyida Nunuu.

It was obvious that I could not stay in Zanzibar without a job. Quite a number of people managed to go to Dar es Salaam where they applied for jobs - and got them. As for me, I thought I would first collect an inheritance from an aunt who had died in Kenya some time ago. As no-one was allowed to leave the Island without permission, I went to the Immigration Office to obtain the required document. Unfortunately, the Immigration Officer commandeered my passport, saying that I was not allowed to leave. I tried to explain to him my reasons for going to Kenya, but he would not listen. On leaving the office, I was advised to seek an interview with the President himself.

Eventually, I was given an appointment to see the President. I explained to him that I wanted to go to Kenya for a few days to receive an inheritance which was overdue. I showed him my file of correspondence with the Registration Office in Kenya and told him that my passport had been confiscated by the Immigration Office. He scrutinised my file and agreed to talk to the Chief Immigration Officer to facilitate my travel.

He added that President Nyerere would give me a job as I was no longer needed in Zanzibar.

Next I went to see the Chief Immigration Officer who said that I would be allowed to travel with a *laisser-passer* (allow to pass) document valid for a month, but then I must return. I left his office full of hope, went home and began to pack my bags. As I did not want to arouse suspicion, I tried to move into our own personal house all the clothes and furniture in the government house that had been ours until the time of the Revolution.

After my departure from Zanzibar I found out that one of the Ministers, in the company of Revolutionary Guards, had gone to my house and forced his way in. The guards searched the entire house and told our African housekeeper that they would come back later and take everything. Then they sealed the doors and left. Our poor, distraught housekeeper was left on the doorstep. She had been with our family since childhood. She also had a son to support. Where would she go?

Without a thought for her own safety, our loyal housekeeper quietly went to the back of the house, climbed up a ladder and went inside. She took the silver cutlery along with other valuable items and hid them somewhere safe for us. When the Minister and his gang of soldiers came back with a truck the next day, they broke the seal on the door and started to clear everything from the rooms. Suddenly they became very angry. "*Where is the silver cutlery? Who has taken it?*" they asked. The housekeeper claimed ignorance of any valuables in the house. She was indeed very brave. The guards were exasperated, but could do nothing. They removed everything left in the house and kept it all for themselves.

While I was preparing to leave the country, my sister decided that she could not remain in Zanzibar either, even though President Karume had been kind enough to allow her to stay in a government house and had agreed to continue to pay her allowance. She felt she would be too lonely after my departure. Sayyida Nunuu had the idea of going to Mombasa where she could observe the situation in Zanzibar from afar, in the hope of returning at a later date.

At last I was ready to leave. After saying goodbye to my sister for the time being, I made my way to Zanzibar Airport. It was reassuring to be able to show my *laisser-passer* as a legitimate travel document. The authorities questioned me rigorously and requested details of my funds. Knowing that people were not allowed to leave the country with lots of money, I had brought only a small sum, but it turned out to be too much, as the customs authorities said I was allowed to keep only forty shillings. I argued that this sum would hardly be enough for me to live on. However, the authorities were adamant. I had no choice but to agree to this unreasonable regulation and I ran back to my driver, who was waiting outside the customs entrance. Reluctantly I gave him the balance. As I boarded the plane my relief was shot through with anxiety. How would I be able to survive on so little money?

I was fortunate in that I had friends in Mombasa who were able to accommodate me, and I stayed with them for some time. Then things took an alarming turn. Word came, via a radio broadcast, to the effect that President Karume was planning to send a ship to Mombasa to arrest us all and take us back to Zanzibar. One can imagine the enormous shock that this was to all Arab Zanzibari refugees in Mombasa. Everyone made arrangements to escape that very night.

Karume claimed that, since we had all left illegally, we must be forced to return. We were very seriously concerned about this sudden turn of events. It was at that point that I made a call to my good friend Prince Badru in Uganda urging him to secure King Kabaka's permission for me and my sister to travel to Kampala and be granted temporary asylum in Uganda. The Prince promised to take up my request with his cousin, the King. We waited for an answer, not knowing our ultimate fate. Would we be allowed to seek asylum in Uganda or would we be returned to

Zanzibar to suffer at the hands of the Rebels? After about an hour the heart-warming reply came - we would be welcome in Uganda! I was tremendously grateful to King Kabaka.

I spent an anxious day planning our journey by train to Uganda. Then news came from an unexpected quarter - President Jomo Kenyatta of Kenya had challenged President Karume's authority to arrest asylum seekers from Zanzibar while they were on Kenyan soil. What crimes had these individuals committed? What evidence did Karume have to prove their guilt?

In a forceful announcement, Kenyatta declared that he would not allow Karume's men to arrest asylum seekers in Kenya. If any evidence were found that crimes had been committed, the Kenyan Police would deal with the matter through proper channels. We were at last able to breathe a collective sigh of relief. I called Prince Badru to tell him how grateful I was to King Kabaka for agreeing to help, but the danger had passed and so I would not need his kind hospitality.

Under the circumstances it was abundantly clear that I must not consider returning to Zanzibar. It was then that I decided to quit East Africa altogether. Leaving the land one loves, the land which has been home for half a century cannot be anything but traumatic, and all the more so when one must take flight under duress, in fact, fearing for one's life. I was extremely fortunate to be able to escape and to have a sheltering place in mind, a safe refuge with family. I was headed for Cairo.

After receiving my inheritance, and despite the fact that I had been offered a job in Kenya, I began my preparations for departure, starting with the necessary travel documents. Before I left, I had a telling meeting with the former British High Commissioner, Mr Timothy Crosthwaite who had just completed his mission of overseeing the Zanzibar Revolution. This included ensuring the safe journey of HH Sultan Jamshid and his family to Dar es Salaam in Tanganyika which had already declared union with Zanzibar - and on to London where they were received as guests of the British Government.

Just before he left Zanzibar for the United Kingdom, Mr Crosthwaite sent a letter to my sister, Sayyida Nunuu in Mombasa, saying he regretted that during his stay in Zanzibar he had not been able to spare the time to visit her. In the letter, Mr Crosthwaite went on to explain that, since he was traveling to London via Mombasa, he would be in town for a few days at the Mombasa Club and hoped to see her. My sister accepted and asked me to guide Mr Crosthwaite and his wife to her residence.

This gave me a chance to talk to the former British High Commissioner. At one point in the conversation, I said that it was a great pity that during the Revolution the British Government did not come to our assistance. My comment was in the context of the fact that when the Tanganyikan army in Dar es Salaam attempted a coup, Nyerere escaped to the British Embassy which was near his palace. A British warship came to Nyerere's aid, an act which signalled the army to return to their barracks.

In reply Crosthwaite said that we wanted independence and it was granted. That meant we were on our own. I said the Zanzibar Sultanate and the British Government had long been friends. I pointed out that the Zanzibaris fought side-by-side with the British in two World Wars when the British needed help in East Africa – and yet the British Government did not help us in return. However, when President Julius Nyerere of Tanganyika needed help against his army who left their barracks to attempt a coup, the British Government instantly sent warships to the harbour and warned the army that they had better return to their barracks - and they did.

Mr Crosthwaite could not reply to this point; but said, or repeated, that President Karume believed that President Nyerere was a good man and would take care of us. It seemed that the two Presidents had discussed the matter. I must say it was surprising that the friendship between the British Government and Zanzibar, which had begun so long ago, should end so abruptly.

151

Despite careful planning, difficulties still lay ahead; I had no travel documents. I decided to seek the help of the British Consul in Mombasa because I had lived in Zanzibar when it was a British Protectorate. I thought that perhaps I could obtain a British passport; however, the British authorities did not respond favourably to my request.

The British Consul stated the facts. As Zanzibar was now an independent nation no longer under British rule, they were unable to grant me a British passport. They were, however, willing to produce a *laisser-passer* document which would allow me to travel to the United Kingdom only. But I was keen to stay close to my children and they were in Cairo. It was for this reason that I was not tempted to seek refuge in England.

I then contacted the immigration authorities in Mombasa with the objective of obtaining a *laisser-passer* to travel to Dubai with a stopover in Cairo. This was granted, but I was told that once I left for Cairo, I would be unable to return to Kenya. It seemed I was on yet another one-way ticket. In December 1964, my sister, Sayyida Nunuu and I, along with Nunuu's adopted daughter, Amal and her child, boarded a plane bound first for Cairo where I would see my children.

The plane arrived late in Nairobi and we all had to run across the tarmac, just making it in time for our connection to Cairo. Unfortunately, we were stopped when the police officer on duty that day recognised Sayyida Nunuu as the late Sultan Sayyid Khalifa's wife, and would not let us board the plane. Uncertain as to whether he should allow members of the Royal Family to travel, the police officer went away to seek confirmation. Meanwhile a planeload of passengers was waiting to take off and the pilot was furious. My sister and I stood as patiently as we could, suppressing the sharp anxiety we both felt, while Amal did not understand what was happening. The tension rose as Amal and her child became increasingly restless. At last the nod of approval was given. The Al Busaidi family was allowed to leave.

Chapter 15
Lucky to be alive

When eventually my sister and I arrived in Cairo, we were received with a very warm welcome and honoured with full hospitality by Samira's mother, Bi Jokha, and her husband, Sheikh Salim bin Saif Al Ma'amari. My former parents-in-law had moved from Zanzibar to Cairo during the 1950's so that their children could receive a better education. When all the children graduated, the family returned to their home in Zanzibar. Early in 1964, as the political situation in Zanzibar began to deteriorate, Sheikh Salim and Bi Johka decided that it was best to go back to Cairo.

The experience of a violent Revolution can never be forgotten, but I remember even more the blessings that came afterwards, especially the kindness of family and friends. I shall never forget how lucky I was to be alive, and how this heightened my appreciation of the way my life unfolded after the Revolution.

I was very grateful to have found a place to stay, but I knew that this could be only a temporary arrangement. Ultimately, I needed to find my own accommodation; and so I began to search for employment. I discussed my situation with my hosts and my sister. Many questions were raised. Should I stay in Cairo or look elsewhere? Although I was advised to stay in Cairo for a while, there were rumours of good opportunities in places like Dubai where I initially had planned to go. I decided to visit the Embassies of all the Gulf States in Cairo, with the hope of finding a job somewhere in the Gulf. I waited for six months, but I did not receive a positive response from any of the Gulf Embassies.

At the same time, the sun shone through all the dark clouds, as it was such a great joy to be reunited with my children. One incident from those days particularly stays in my mind. Although my second child,

Rawya, was only a young girl at the time, she was extremely concerned about my situation. One day, Rawya came home from school to say that she had mentioned my predicament to her one of her classmates, the daughter of a wealthy Saudi Arabian businessman who owned an electricity plant in the Kingdom. Rawya wondered if there was a possibility of a job for me there. I was deeply touched by my young daughter's attempt to help me find work. She arranged for me to meet with the businessman at our residence in Madinat Al Muhandisin. The meeting went very well and the man promised to look into the matter on his return to Saudi Arabia.

All of a sudden my plans changed when, unexpectedly, an Egyptian gentleman named Mr Fatthi Awadh came to visit Bi Jokha. He had known the family when he was a small child and had happy memories of those days. When Mr Awadh heard that Bi Jokha was back in town, he decided to drop by for a visit. It came up in conversation that Mr Awadh was planning to go to Libya to seek employment.

Immediately, Bi Jokha suggested that I go with him. Fatthi Awadh was delighted at the idea of having a companion for the long and arduous journey across the vast, open desert from Cairo to Tripoli. I casually asked him when he was planning to leave and he shocked me by saying he was going the very next day! So, after a frantic rush to pack and prepare for my departure, I left Cairo with Mr Awadh in his big Mercedes Benz, accompanied by the same Mohamed Masoud Al Riyami with whom I had shared that otherwise dreadful night in jail and who also had fled to Cairo.

The three of us travelled overland, through the seemingly unending desert, towards Marsa Matruh on the Egyptian-Libyan border, passing derelict tanks and the ruins of crashed war planes along the way. As we approached the border crossing, anxiety crept up on me like a stealthy assailant in the night. The question going through my head was, "*Will*

I be allowed to proceed? " I had no proper passport, only a *laisser-passer* attached to a 'passport' issued by the 'Oman Imamate in Exile in Cairo.' This documentation was supposed to be accepted by most Arab countries, but I could not be sure.

The other problem I anticipated at the border was with respect to money. I had changed currency on the black market, which I knew was considered illegal. Would the border police confiscate my money? Mr Awadh had already warned us that, if for any reason we were barred from entering Libya, he would have to continue without us. I wondered what we would do if we found ourselves stuck at the border without money or transportation. I just prayed that all would be well.

My heart was pounding as the officer on duty scrutinized my papers with a severe frown upon his face. Eventually he looked me in the eye and asked, "*Are you from Zanzibar?* " I nodded as confidently as I could. Did this mean I would not be allowed to cross the border? The officer suddenly threw my papers down on the counter and walked away. Minutes passed. I continued to pray, realising that the official's decision would be crucial to my future. Thankfully, everything appeared to be in order, and in spite of his dramatic gesture with my papers, the officer allowed us to cross the border.

My two companions and I jumped back into the car and Fatthi Awadh drove as fast as the car would safely go until we reached the large Italian-built town of Benghazi on the Mediterranean coast. Our benefactor suddenly announced his intention to stay in Benghazi for a while. Mohammed and I were dismayed, but had no option but to comply with his wishes. We found a cheap *pensione*, or small guest house, and stayed there while we searched for work since our money was slowly running out. It wasn't long before Mr Awadh dropped the bombshell - he had decided to stay in Benghazi and would not be able to drive us to Tripoli. Now what would we do?

Left stranded, we were still determined to reach the capital. The best option was not particularly inviting - a long overnight bus journey to Tripoli. The bus was overloaded with passengers who were packed like sardines into seats and cheek-by-jowl in the aisle. And so it was an extremely uncomfortable and tiring journey, but we arrived safe and sound in Tripoli the next morning. Fortunately, Samira had found a job in Tripoli as an Inspector of English at a local girls' school and she and the children were already settled in. By the time I had paid the taxi fare to Samira's house, my wallet was pretty well empty. What a relief it was to finally be standing on Samira's front door and to see our children again in the comfort of and safety of their home.

It was towards the end of 1964 when I arrived in Tripoli. Right away I wrote a letter to the Libyan Minister of Finance, Mr Al Baruni, whom my former brother-in-law, Mohammed Salem Al Ma'amari, had met in London. This was a very good connection as the Minister's father, Sheikh Suleiman Al Baruni, was a tribal leader and a highly respected Ibadhi scholar. Years before, he had disagreed with the American and British installation of the monarchy in Libya. Suleiman Al Buruni had many followers and the British authorities thought that he might cause trouble. King Senussi, the former Libyan ruler, was far more popular in Benghazi than he was in Tripoli. Rumour had it that, during World War II, the Senussi Bedu had helped the British when their planes were hit by the Germans in the desert. Senussi's followers rescued the British airmen and secretly took them by camel to Egypt.

When the famous German Field Marshall, General Erwin Rommel, popularly known as 'Desert Fox', asked the local Bedu about the whereabouts of the missing British airmen, they pretended they did not know, although they were actually the very same Bedu who had escorted the British airmen across the desert to safety. The British authorities were naturally grateful to Senussi and, accordingly, they felt

156

indebted. It is said that the British were instrumental in the manoeuvers that resulted in Senussi's installation as King Idris I of Libya in 1951.

Suleiman Al Baruni was one of those who objected to Senussi's enthronement. The British promptly arrested Sheikh Suleiman and determined that he should be deported, but allowed him to choose his country of exile. Oman was the country that the Sheikh chose for asylum and when the British authorities approached Sultan Said bin Taimur for permission, it was granted. A British warship took Sheikh Suleiman Al Baruni to Oman; his family was to follow.

After some time in Muscat, Sheikh Suleiman decided to settle in Nizwa where he made many contacts and worked for the betterment of the country. According to information I got from Tripoli, Sheikh Suleiman urged Omanis in the interior to open schools to educate their children. Apparently he got results because one community did undertake to build a school. But, unfortunately, while in Nizwa, Sheikh Suleiman suffered a severe case of food poisoning. Since he could not get proper medical treatment in Oman, the family boarded a boat to take him to India. Sadly, Sheikh Suleiman Al Baruni died during the voyage.

I went to see Sheikh Suleiman's son, the Libyan Minister, Mr Al Baruni, and explained my situation to him and my need for employment. The Minister very kindly discussed this matter with the authority of the Libyan Tobacco Company, laying the groundwork for me. With a letter of introduction from the Minister, I managed to get a job as Transport Officer in the Tobacco Company and immediately started to work.

The factory had originally been built by the Italians during their rule of Libya. Although the business still employed Italian technicians, it was operated by British-American Tobacco Company staff. I felt at home with an Englishman I met at the factory who had lived in Tanganyika and spoke Swahili very well. We would often chat together in Swahili. Among my Libyan colleagues was Mr Mohamed Abdulla Baguba, a kind man, and Mr Abdulla Naas who often came to see me in my office. The European staff included Mr Skidmore, a friendly gentleman who was very understanding.

I was extremely relieved not only to have found work and a measure of stability, but also a congenial social environment. Many Zanzibaris from abroad contacted me, enquiring about the possibility of work in Libya, and soon a stream of fellow Zanzibaris began to arrive. Nevertheless, life in Libya was markedly different to what they and I had grown accustomed to in Zanzibar, a place that now seemed a distant dream.

Obviously, I had to make a huge adjustment to fit into unfamiliar surroundings in a new career and lifestyle. At the same time there were many attractions. I enjoyed the city of Tripoli with its Mediterranean climate and inspiring views of the island of Sicily across the sparkling waters of that vast blue sea, famous from the epics of Homer.

I found the Libyans to be good people who are reserved with strangers until they get to know them. They appeared to be healthy and strong, enjoying an excellent climate with only one uncomfortable month - in summer when the desert wind, full of dust, blows north across the country, reaching as far as the coast of Italy. When this wind, known as 'Gibli', comes, people stay indoors as much as possible. The air is difficult to breathe and visibility is poor.

I have heard lots of stories about the Italian occupation and the cruelty that Libyans endured, some of which cannot be printed on these pages. A persistent story was that some of the Libyans who rose in protest against repressive and cruel treatment were apparently taken over the ocean in airplanes and dropped from a height at which no human being can survive.

During the Italian regime, the Libyans felt humiliated. Their children were badly educated because government schools were at a low standard and schooling stopped at the end of the primary level. Libyans were told that their children did not need any further schooling - it was enough that they could sign their names. Libyans who worked in construction were subjected to an Italian superior who would stand by with a whip - and apparently he would use it. Because of such horrendous treatment, Libyans came to view all foreigners with suspicion, and so they tend not to trust any strangers, whatever nationality they might be.

When I started my new life in Libya, I was naturally concerned about the education of my children. However Rayyan was top of her class and stood first among all students at Tripoli College where she was studying at the secondary level. The College was so impressed with Rayyan's ability that they offered her a scholarship to any school of her choice. Without a moment's hesitation, Rayyan chose to go back to Alice Oatley School in England.

Education was a top priority for all our children. Rawya studied at school in Cairo, at college in Tripoli, at Baghdad University for her Bachelor of Science degree, and at Kings College, University of London where she completed a Masters in Education. It was at the University of Oxford that Rawya crowned her many years of study, earning a Doctorate of Philosophy in Science Education.

My son, Ahmed was a serious student, but had quite a disrupted school education - first in Zanzibar, then Cairo and Libya. Eventually, Samira took Ahmed to England and registered him in a good boarding school. Later, Ahmed went to Saint Louis University in the USA, where he graduated with a BSc in Computer Science. In recent times, as a mature student, Ahmed was awarded an MBA with high standing from the University of Hull.

With my daughter, Rawya, at her graduation from the University of Oxford

What seemed at first to be a temporary arrangement in Libya lasted seven years. And so it was that I lived with fellow Arabs and my Omani-Zanzibari compatriots in a country I probably would never have known otherwise. Those years were full of wonderful encounters with people from my old homeland. While the stories of these meetings are simple ones, I hope they express how full the human heart can be from small acts of kindness in this world where there is far more to be thankful for, than not.

During my years in Libya, from time to time I would travel to Jeddah with my children to visit my sister, Sayyida Nunuu, who was happily settled there, thanks to King Faisal, God bless his soul. The first time we went to Jeddah, the address that my sister had given me was not sufficient for the taxi driver to locate the house. After driving all over town, the taxi driver took us to a hotel where he thought we might get help in locating the area where my sister lived.

As I stood at the reception desk, I noticed some of the staff looking at me intently. When I spoke to my children in Swahili, the porter heard the sound of the language and rushed to take my hand and greet me. He said he had thought from the beginning that I was from Zanzibar, and excitedly called the hotel staff to greet me. I discovered that they were all Zanzibaris! Most of them remembered me, as they were born and bred in Malindi, close to my old house in Zanzibar.

When I explained my problem in trying to find my sister's house, they said they had heard that she was somewhere in Jeddah and assured me that there would be no problem in finding her. One of them rang Sheikh Mohammed bin Salim Al Ruwahi who told me he knew where my sister was, but said he must first take me to his house for coffee. He arrived at the hotel within minutes.

161

In spite of the urgency, the good Sheikh would not let me go straight to my sister. So my children and I suppressed our impatience and went home with Sheikh Mohammed for coffee. We ended up very much enjoying this pleasant interlude. Eventually Sheikh Mohammed took us to my sister's house. Dear Nunuu had been expecting me for some time and was very worried. Oh, what a great joy it was for all of us to meet, having parted so long ago!

On one occasion, when I was in Saudi Arabia visiting my sister, I seized the opportunity to go to Mecca for *umra,* a shorter, more informal version of the famous hajj pilgrimage in which faithful Muslims perform religious rituals centred on the Ka'ba and Mount Arafat. As my children, Rayyan, Rawya and Ahmed were with me at the time, we were able to complete the *umra* together - an unforgettable experience that brought us closer as a family.

I had been in Tripoli for five years when suddenly I found myself caught up in yet another Revolution. King Idris, the reigning monarch of Libya, was ailing and unable to cope effectively with the heavy demands of political life. It was said that his wife and one senior army officer were virtually running the country on his behalf. When the King travelled to Italy for medical treatment, the army took the opportunity to usurp him and take control of the country.

On 1st September 1969, I was following my normal routine of driving to work early in the morning. However, I soon realized that something was very wrong as the streets of Tripoli were eerily silent and empty. Just as I was passing the British Embassy, an army truck, carrying several soldiers, swerved to a halt right in front of me and a soldier yelled out, "*Who are you? What do you think you are doing here? Don't you know there's a Revolution going on? There's no work today! Go home and stay there!*"

I immediately turned the car around and headed for home. The army truck actually followed me to my house, making me extremely nervous. As I entered the building and went to look out of the window, a soldier shouted out to me, "*Shut the window!*" I stayed at home all day, fearful of a replay of the violent events that I had witnessed in Zanzibar just five years earlier. However, the Libyan Revolution turned out to be a bloodless coup. A young, religious army officer by the name of Colonel Qaddafi had taken control of the country. Following the coup, I learned that the many corrupt officials who had lined their pockets under the King's rule were ousted from their positions by the new military regime.

Less than a year later, another dramatic change of leadership in the Arab world, this time in the Gulf, would herald a new era. That momentous and historic event would have a far greater effect on my life.

The Author with HE Sayyid Mohamed bin Ahmed al Busaidi, Minister of Interior

Chapter 16
Great Expectations fulfilled

During my seven-year sojourn in Tripoli, I would meet regularly with other Zanzibaris, and the conversation often turned to politics. What everyone was talking about on the 23rd of July 1970, was the sudden rise to power of a young Prince, Sultan Qaboos bin Said, who succeeded his father, Sultan Said bin Taimur as Sovereign of what was then known as 'Muscat and Oman' and would soon become the Sultanate of Oman.

This Sandhurst-educated, blue-blooded scion of the Al bu Said Dynasty was ready to lead his country into the dawn of a new era. I remember how we all felt on that momentous day, a day that was destined to become the most significant in the modern history of the Sultanate. We were incredibly excited about this dramatic change and what it might mean for us.

With an energetic young ruler who had lived abroad, we were sure that the people of Oman could look forward to a much better life. We wanted to be part of what would later be known as Oman's Renaissance. We ardently hoped that, at last, we would be able to return to our ancestral home.

We were not disappointed. The long-closed doors of Oman were opened wide. With wisdom and expedience, His Majesty Sultan Qaboos bin Said welcomed all overseas Omanis to return to their ancestral home. This exciting news caused Omanis everywhere to raise their hands and thank God for their deliverance.

An untold number of Omanis from Zanzibar had suffered tremendously. There were countless stories of extreme deprivation. Those unfortunate people who had stowed away on animal cargo ships where they hid

The Author at work in the Ministry of Interior

Mr Habib Shushtary, my good friend from Zanzibar (p. 186)

among the cattle and goats in straw and filth, had suffered dehydration and starvation. Others were dumped by dhows on the shores of the Arabian Gulf in extreme heat without food or water. Sadly, some of those so shockingly abandoned were never to realize their dreams. They simply perished.

Hundreds of people who left Zanzibar in the aftermath of the Revolution arrived without money or travel documents. The authorities in the Arabian Gulf knew little about the suffering of these Arab kinsmen, or the hardship and danger they had endured. I think some Gulf States may have been advised not to welcome Zanzibari Omanis because of the suspicion that they brought with them the threat of Communism.

During that difficult period, only Sheikh Rashid, the Ruler of Dubai realized that Zanzibari Omanis were actually running away from communist tyranny and were certainly not communists themselves. In a wonderful humanitarian act, Sheikh Rashid Al Maktoum welcomed Zanzibari Omanis to the UAE. This generous Ruler even went so far as to build houses in an area called Rashidia for the refugees with whom he sympathised as fellow Arabs.

Some time after the earth-shattering news about His Majesty Sultan Qaboos bin Said, I read an article in a Libyan newspaper regarding a delegation from Oman that would soon arrive in Tripoli. His Majesty had dispatched members of his new Government to tour the capitals of Arab nations in order to inform them about his accession to the throne and to convey his sincere wish to promote good will and improve relations throughout the Arab world in a genuine spirit of friendship.

Understandably, we were all keen to meet with members of the delegation – so much so that we found out where they were staying and ventured to the hotel. The members of the delegation, led by Mohammed bin Suleiman Al Taie whose son later became Editor-in-

Chief of Oman's Tribune newspaper, were surprised to find that we were living in Tripoli. They enquired about the problems we had faced in Zanzibar in 1964, and wanted to know about our lives in Libya. We, in turn, were keen to find out more about His Majesty Sultan Qaboos bin Said and the many great changes planned for the Sultanate. They told us of His Majesty's announcement that all Omanis, and all those of Omani origin, would be welcome to return to the Sultanate to help develop the country.

Knowing that the Zanzibari Omanis working in Libya were educated and experienced, the delegation offered us the opportunity to live and work in Oman. His Majesty's vision was of a modern nation and it had to be built from scratch. People with knowledge and expertise were required to develop Oman's dormant economy, to create a physical infrastructure and to put in place modern services, especially for health, education, social services and communication.

So it was, that in 1971, I packed my bags once again, leaving Tripoli to start a new life in Oman. My Libyan friends had tried to dissuade me, saying that I would be sorely missed in Libya. In fact they promised that, if I changed my mind, they would try to obtain Libyan citizenship for me, but they cautioned that if I left, and things did not turn out well in Oman, it might be difficult for me to return. However, I was determined to seize this great opportunity finally to travel to the home of my forefathers. I had heard so much about Oman from my grandfather that it became an enduring theme in my thoughts, as if the country had always been part of my psyche. Now, at last, I would be able to see Oman with my own eyes and start a new and better life as a true national. I would no longer be a foreigner in a land that could never be mine.

I will never forget the day I flew into the airport at Wadi Al Kabir near Muscat. I was struck by the stark beauty of the Hajar Mountains against the pure blue of the sky and sea, with clusters of white houses nestled in small bays along the shore and in the sheltered valleys. It seemed a peaceful and inviting place.

By chance, I met an old friend, Sayyid Hamoud Saud Al Said, at the airport who was kind enough to take me home in his car. We entered the walled city of Muscat through Bab Al Kabir, an imposing gate with great wooden doors, beyond which was the apartment where I would live, close to the offices of Sayyid Hamed bin Hamoud.

I remember how I marvelled at the new royal residence on Muscat Harbour, the Al Alam Palace, which was then under construction at the order of His Majesty Sultan Qaboos bin Said. Fittingly, this distinctive blue and gold palace is overlooked by two ancient forts, Al Mirani and Al Jalali. Stationed high on the mountain cliffs on either side of the Harbour, the two majestic forts stand guard above the emerald waters, just as they have for the past five centuries. Until recently, cannon were fired from Al Mirani to announce the beginning and end of each day.

After settling into my new environment, I was advised by HH Sayyid Faher bin Taimur Al Said, whom I had met earlier during his visit to Tripoli, to see my cousin, Sayyid Hilal bin Hamed Al Busaidi, the Wali of Sohar. Sayyid Faher kindly provided me with a Land Rover and a driver for the long journey to Sohar. At the time, there was only a graded dirt road to Sohar which meant several long uncomfortable hours as we bumped along, trying to avoid the huge potholes that punctuated the road like small craters.

There were some very pleasant surprises in store for me upon arrival in Sohar. My cousin came out to greet me personally and very kindly invited me to stay for a few days so that that we might get to know each other. I was to be accommodated in the Great Fort of Sohar! This

169

'hotel' was definitely different! That night I was the guest of honour at a special dinner of goat meat and rice on which we feasted while sitting cross-legged on the floor of the fort.

I was overjoyed to be in the country of my ancestors and to meet my cousin, Sayyid Hilal, at long last. At the first opportunity I went to visit Barka, the home of my ancestors. Just before my grandfather died, he reminisced about his house in Barka, and I had set my heart on seeing it. Unfortunately, I found that only the outer wall, the façade and front door of the old family house were still standing. Still it seemed to evoke the aura of my ancestors and it was wonderful to walk around the village about which I had heard so much.

My family had been in this area for some time. I know that my grandmother was born and bred nearby at Al Felaij Castle. I was told that, as a young girl, she would look out of her window to watch the horses which were tethered in the yard. She loved it when a rider would come, mount his horse and gallop off into the distance.

One fine day, as my wistful grandmother was watching the beautiful horses from her window and no-one was in sight, she had an irresistible impulse to ride. The young lady gathered her courage, ran outdoors, jumped on a horse, and galloped off at high speed in a cloud of dust! Unfortunately, my grandmother did not know how to ride. Within minutes, the young rider's exhilaration changed to brutal shock as she was violently thrown off the speeding horse and went crashing to the ground. My grandmother was brought back to the castle virtually unconscious, but lived to tell the tale!

During my first weeks in Oman, I was advised to visit HH Sayyid Thuwaini bin Taimur - and I did. It was very interesting to meet with this gracious personage, a top official and member of the Royal Family. HH Sayyid Faher was kind enough also to introduce me to HH Sayyid Fahd bin Mahmoud bin Turki, the Minister of Foreign Affairs as I wanted to serve in that Ministry. Following a successful interview, I was fortunate enough to embark upon a new career - in Oman's Foreign Service.

Almost as soon as I joined the Ministry of Foreign Affairs in 1972, I was sent to Oman's Embassy in Tehran as Second Secretary. I was thrilled with this appointment in an important capital in the region, a city that would be of great interest to me because of its history and the unknown possibilities it might present. I did not expect to meet anyone in Tehran whom I knew, but to my amazement, an old neighbour from Malindi in Zanzibar, Mr Habib Shushtary, walked into the Embassy one day. He was most hospitable, taking me to his house to meet his wife, Aughra and their two children, Katy and Ramy. I felt very much at home with this family and was no longer a stranger in Tehran.

I served under the leadership of Mr Al Rasasi, Oman's first Ambassador to Iran. It was a wonderful posting. I loved the rich and diverse landscape of Iran and the many different nationalities that I encountered in the cosmopolitan city of Tehran. The diplomatic community was very active, and I was keen to attend the numerous professional and social functions to which I was invited. This multicultural milieu afforded me an opportunity to learn a great deal about many of the countries and cultures represented.

One of my responsibilities in Tehran included receiving delegations at the airport. His Majesty Sultan Qaboos paid a state visit to Iran during my tenure. I believe the year of his visit was 1974. The Embassy arranged a quite magnificent luncheon for clerics in honour of His Majesty. That evening the Shah, Mohammed Reza Pahlavi, invited HM Sultan Qaboos bin Said and his delegation to a banquet at the Sadabad Palace.

Following the banquet, there was a wonderful play to entertain the royal guests and their retinues. The sets portrayed a beautiful garden

171

where what appeared to be a real deer wandered around. A handsome Prince arrived and proceeded to hunt the deer with his bow and arrow. Suddenly, and much to the delight of the audience, the deer was transformed into a beautiful woman. It was truly an enchanting vening – far removed from the simmering troubles of the country.

I was well aware of the political tensions that were building up in Iran during the 1970's. I believe one of the reasons was rooted in what seemed to me the enormous discrepancy between the rich and the poor. Despite agrarian reform, food prices were climbing ever higher, but most people lacked the courage to complain. The Shah's secret police force and intelligence service, the infamous SAVAK, had created a tangible climate of fear. Once, when I was in the souq, I remember hearing a man desperately shouting, "*I'm hungry! Please help me, I need something to eat!*" Everyone tried to curtail the man's outburst as no-one wanted the dreaded *SAVAK* to arrive.

Empress Farah tried to help by establishing a committee to oversee controls on the price of food. Every morning there was a radio announcement dictating the cost of various foods. However, shopkeepers did not always adhere to these directives. One day in the souq, I came across a group of angry people standing outside a butcher's shop. They had found that the butcher's meat prices were far higher than the price of meat announced in the morning broadcast.

When the butcher heard the complaints from his customers, he said, "*If you want the prices announced on the radio, well then, you should go and buy your meat at the radio station!*" The people were incensed. Obviously there was corruption, as it soon transpired that the butcher's shop was actually owned by one of the Iranian Ministers!

Injustice and inequity characterised the health services provided for the people. There was only one Government hospital in Tehran at that time, and all the private hospitals were ruthless in their treatment of those desperately in need of their services. If a person badly injured in an accident were taken to the nearest hospital, the medical staff would refuse to assist unless the fees were paid in advance. People literally bled to death on the street if they could not afford to pay. I think this was what prompted Empress Farah to set up a committee to tackle poverty and corruption.

Meanwhile, the people's hero, Ayatollah Khomeini, was living in exile in France. Cassettes of his speeches were smuggled into Iran, and people would congregate secretly in private houses to listen to Khomeini's speeches which invariably condemned the Shah and his Government.

I met the Shah on several occasions. I felt that the Emperor had indeed lost touch with his people. The Shah was in his own isolated 'ivory tower' and did not seem to be aware of the difficulties that the majority of people in Iran were facing. He apparently did not detect the rumblings of discontent among his people. Remembering that one of the great lessons of history is that when a monarch loses meaningful contact with his people, the health of the nation is at risk, I wrote to my Government in Muscat to tell them of my concerns for Iran.

I did not witness the last stages of the Shah's reign, as by then I was posted elsewhere. Apparently the Shah, who was no longer well and looked haggard, eventually went to South America where a specialist French physician came from Paris to treat him. Early in January of 1979 when, unknown to the Shah, political discontent was coming to a head, he again left the country for medical treatment. No sooner was the Shah out of the country than the Iranian Revolution broke out and he was forever barred from the centuries-old royal seat of Persia. The dynasty that his father established in 1925, after usurping the Qajar monarchy in an earlier military coup, lasted little more than a half century.

As the world knows, Ayatollah Khomeini returned to Iran from exile in France to a hero's welcome. Surprisingly, the Shah was refused asylum in America and most European countries as well. The ailing Emperor was eventually given asylum in Egypt where he arrived on the 16th of January, 1979. Shah Mohammed Reza Pahlavi died a year and a half later and was buried in Cairo on the 29th of July, 1980.

In 1975, I was given a new posting in our Embassy in Doha, Qatar. The Emir, Khalifa bin Hammad Al Thani, had been ruling the country since 1972. In the 1970's the Qatari Ministry of Foreign Affairs was run by just a few people as, of course, Qatar was not the modern country that it is today. Oman's Ambassador to Qatar was Sheikh Ahmed Al Nabhani. I must say that I very much enjoyed working under Ambassador Al Nabhani, a fine diplomat and accomplished leader. I found him to be broad-minded, perceptive and understanding.

That was my last posting overseas. I was then privileged to continue serving my Government in-country.

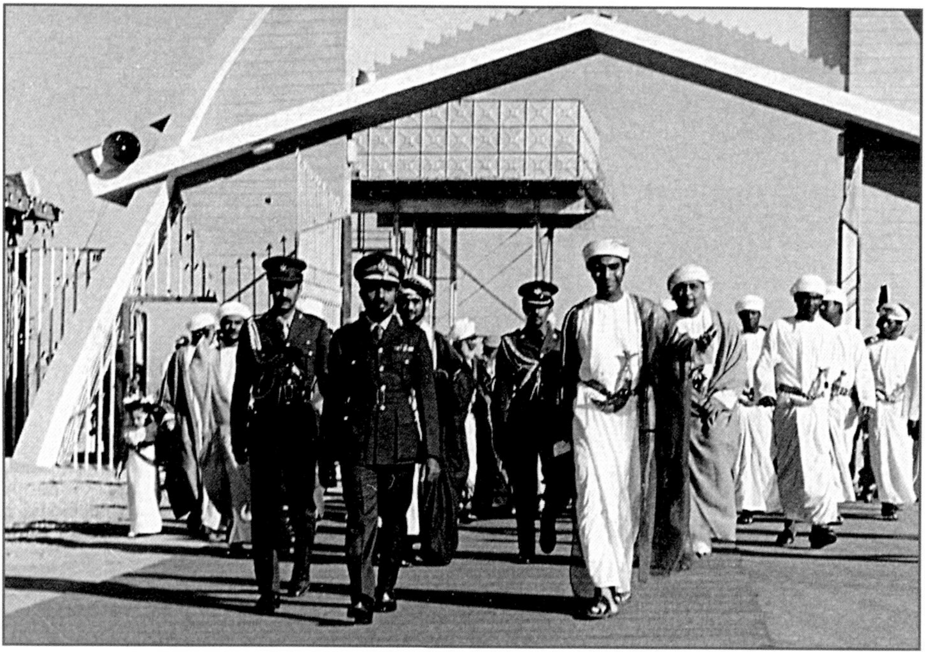

Al Roya Archive

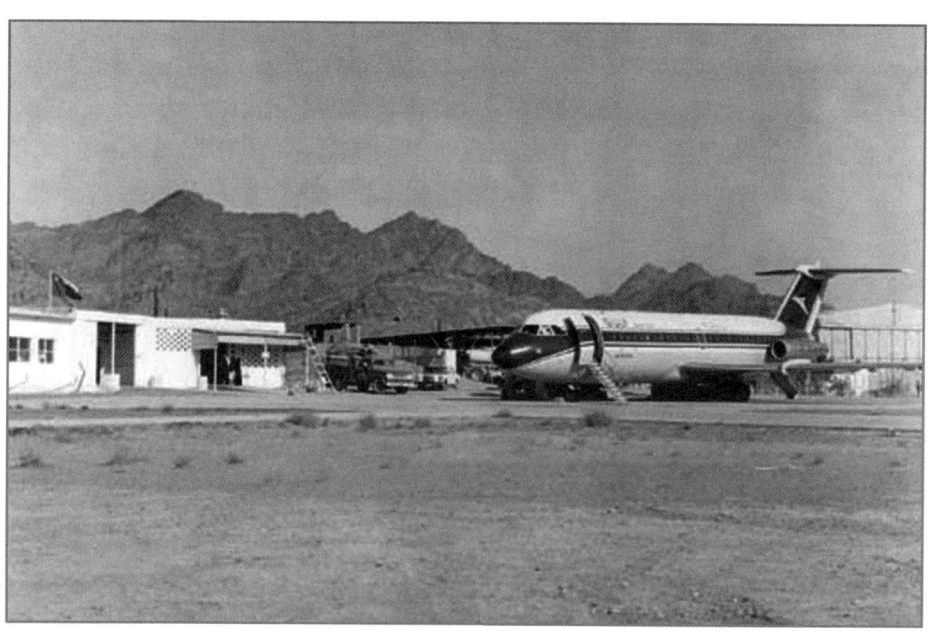

HM Sultan Qaboos bin Said with Sayyid Fahad, Sayyid Tariq and Mohammed Al Zubair in 1973

Al Roya Archive

The Airport in Ruwi where the Author first set foot in Oman

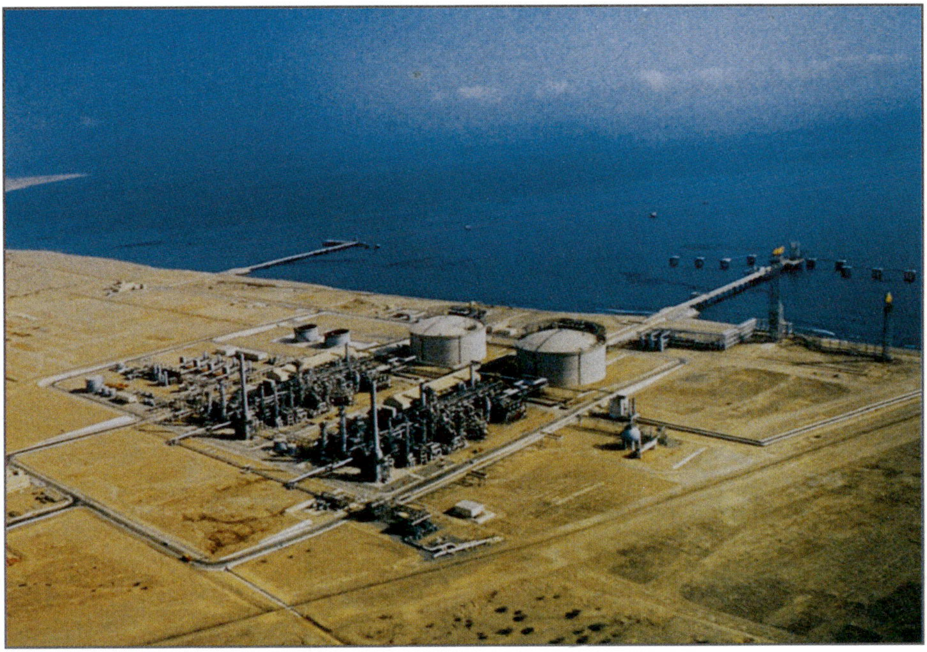

Al Roya Archive

Oman's first oil refinery

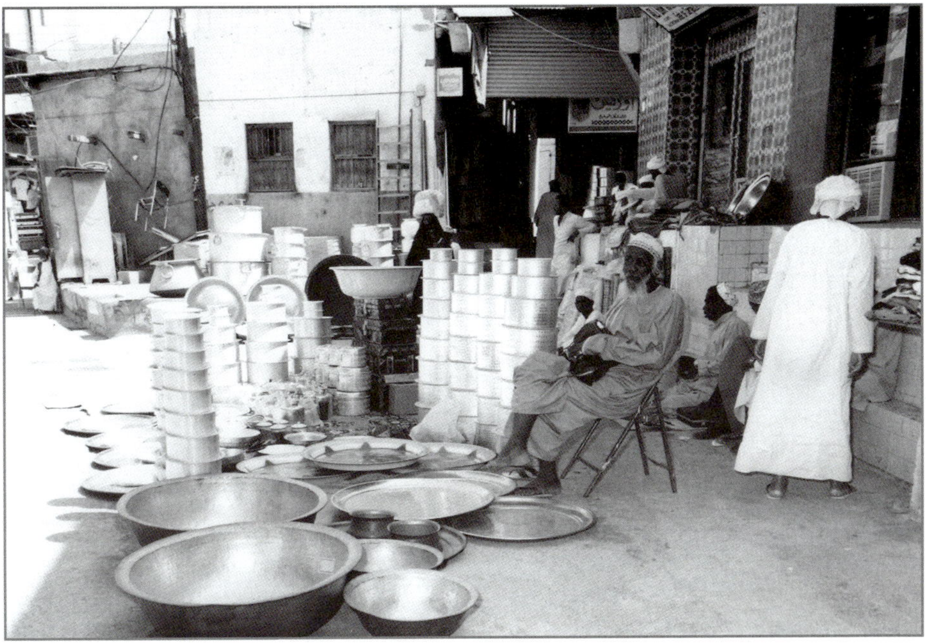

Al Roya Archive

Mutrah Souq in the 1970s

Chapter 17
Reflections on Oman's Renaissance

Returning to Muscat in 1976 on completion of my diplomatic sojourn abroad, I was able to witness first-hand the rapid and thorough transformation that was in progress under the direction of His Majesty Sultan Qaboos bin Said. This was to be a reform of unparalleled scope and intensity, which I believe will receive greater recognition on the world stage as the Sultanate becomes better known internationally. Quite literally, the country was pulled up by its bootstraps from a semi-feudal condition straight into the space age.

Much has been written about this miraculous transformation in the local and regional media, as well as abroad, most prominently in business magazines in London and New York, and I would like to bring a personal perspective to the growing body of reports. I feel that it is fitting for the penultimate chapter in my memoirs to be a tribute to the country that gave me not only identity and a lasting home, but hope for the future.

I greatly admired the new Sultan's style of governing. Right from the start, HM Sultan Qaboos bin Said demonstrated a deep commitment to his people and to his country. I clearly remember the National Day speech eloquently delivered by His Majesty, in which he outlined a series of five year plans designed to accelerate Oman's social and economic development.

I believe the Sultanate was able to make such remarkable progress not only because of His Majesty's wisdom and far-sighted vision, but also because of his down-to-earth approach. Every year His Majesty would embark on a 'Meet the People' tour in which he travelled by car, often behind the wheel, to various regions so that he could see conditions with his own eyes. In this way, the HM Sultan was easily accessible to his people and personally aware of the difficulties they were facing. The Walis of each region would come and talk to His Majesty about the problems and needs of their communities. Ordinary people came too, and His Majesty would listen intently to their concerns.

In my role at the Ministry of Interior, I took part in some of the exciting work of the Renaissance. Infrastructure, health and education had become the top priorities. When I first arrived in 1971, there were only a few kilometres of tarmac in the entire country. A comprehensive modern network of roads now connects cities, towns and settlements throughout the country. Road construction has always been difficult and expensive in Oman as it often involves engineering solutions for flood protection in wadi plains and cutting though mountainous areas. Nevertheless, even remote villages in wilderness areas, or on high cliffs, were connected by road to the main arteries. Quite literally, if mountains had to be moved, they were.

Education was another tremendous challenge. To my knowledge, in the time before Sultan Qaboos bin Said, there was only one secular school in Muscat. That school was for boys only. By the year 2000, there were hundreds of schools all over the country. In the early days, to the great delight and trepidation of school children, His Majesty would often visit schools, actually enter the classroom and talk to students, asking them about their studies.

In 1977, the Sultan's School, a private bilingual school for outstanding students was opened. In 1980, His Majesty encouraged all those involved in the Sultan's School, or hoping to be, by personally endowing a number of scholarships for students without means. There were no universities in those days. In fact, there were very few opportunities for Higher Education. This was soon remedied. In 1986, Oman's first higher education institution, Sultan Qaboos University, opened its doors to 500 students. Barely a decade later, in 2005, there were more than 10,000 students attending the University and thousands of others enrolled in a new system of private universities and colleges. The higher education system would grow to well over 80,000 students in more than sixty colleges and universities by the end of the first decade of the twenty-first century.

At the same time as the education system was growing apace, a national heath care system was rapidly evolving. In the early 1970's there were only two hospitals - the Mission Hospital in Muscat, and Al Nadha Hospital in Ruwi. In 1974, Khoula Hospital was built by PDO (Petroleum Development Oman) for its employees. This hospital was later transferred to the Ministry of Health.

A state-of-the-art government hospital, the Royal Hospital, opened its doors in 1987. Next, the Sultan Qaboos University Hospital was established as a teaching hospital with first class facilities. Thanks to His Majesty's commitment to the health and welfare of his people, by 2004, there were enough hospitals to serve the country's needs. Clinics and health centres were built throughout the country to augment the hospital system, ensuring that every citizen, near and far, had access to free health care.

During the early years of his reign, His Majesty Sultan Qaboos would always take a personal interest in building projects, often visiting construction sites and talking to the workers. I particularly remember the keen interest His Majesty took in the construction of the Al Bustan Palace Hotel in the 1980's.

This new five star hotel represented a watershed, as there were few hotels back in the 1970's and none at an international standard. We used to have dinner at the Gulf Hotel, now the Crowne Plaza, or the Al Falaj Hotel in Ruwi. Guests staying in the Al Falaj would often be placed in a room with other guests. It was more like a dormitory! By the mid 1970's with the oil boom, visitors began to pour into Muscat and, to meet the demand, a new high-rise hotel was built on the pristine sand dunes of Shatti Al Qu'rum – the Muscat Intercontinental. It stood like a giant beacon on the plain as there were no other buildings in the area at that time.

Fortunately for the Sultanate, with its enlightened Head of State, no stone has been left unturned in the effort to provide education for the people. In addition to the scores of thousands studying in-country, over fourteen thousand students are studying abroad for a grand total of more than a hundred thousand Omanis in higher education. Thus the Government is ensuring that that new generations are prepared for the responsible work that lies ahead in contributing substantively to the development of the nation.

Apart from the knowledge gained in higher education, experience is required and that takes time. A country does not reach maturity overnight. When we admire expatriate expertise, we have to remember how long it took for developed countries to reach the point of being able to export skills and expertise. The developed world went through a great deal of trial and error and many generations of students before they reached their present high standard of education.

Oman is very lucky to be blessed with oil. It is well understood that our reserves of oil could come to an end one day - and I am proud that this state of affairs was recognised by His Majesty. He and his Government have taken action to find other ways of generating wealth so that the country will not be totally reliant on income from oil and gas production. It is diversification of the economy that will ensure our future. Industry is now flourishing, but I feel that agricultural development has been slow.

As an Omani, I most certainly have a great love for my country, but I don't think it is wrong to criticize certain practices. I believe that constructive criticism can alert the authorities to problems and help them find remedies. Most developed countries have gained a tolerance for constructive criticism because of the belief that people and systems are not infallible. Well-intentioned criticism stimulates government to review the past, correct mistakes and proactively improve systems. It is in this way, and with sustained motivation, that progress is achieved. I dare say that we Arabs have been known for a certain lack of motivation and a hesitance to be proactive. This has cost us dearly.

I will elaborate on this point by using an analogy. There is an old African story about the importance of acting in a timely manner. The people of a certain village began to complain to their Chief because his dog was attacking their pets and chickens. They endured the situation for some time as no-one would control the dog because it wore the Chief's collar. The Chief would not listen to his people. Instead, he simply told the village elders that everything was fine because the dog and the villagers were all his subjects. Eventually the villagers lodged a much more serious complaint, as the dog had grown larger and more savage. Like a wild animal, the beastly dog was attacking their children.

Again, the chief refused to take action. One day the Chief's dog went into a nursery where it attacked and killed a baby. That baby happened to be the newly born child of the Chief. Arriving in the middle of a great commotion, the horrified Chief saw what had happened to his baby. Instantly, he drew his sword and killed the dog. The people were both saddened and relieved. They bemoaned the situation, saying if only the Chief had taken timely action, the baby would be alive.

As important as the economy and politics are, heritage and culture are also at the top of the agenda for both the government and people of Oman. The roots of the nation are in trading, seafaring, fishing, herding and oasis agriculture. While trading is now mainly a corporate venture, small transactions remain the lifeblood of souqs. Small fishing boats still leave village shores each morning for the daily catch. Goats, and sometimes sheep, are a feature of every interior settlement, and farmers still tend small plots and orchards in fertile wadi plains and on terraced mountain cliffs.

The culture of the desert Bedouin remains a strong influence and the camel still plays a central role in the cultural life of the nation. Camel races are an enduring tradition in the countryside and are always an important component of Eid festivities. Exciting displays of the Royal

Camel Cavalry are featured in His Majesty's famous 'Tattoo' or military band parade. It is interesting to note that some Muscat residents still keep camels. Knowing they cannot rear their camels in the city, they raise camels on farms outside the city. On weekends they go to their farms to talk to their camels and just to be with them.

As Arabs from desert lands who have long relied on the camel, we believe that these animals are endowed with a high degree of intelligence. They are also very sociable. I remember one day arriving at a house on the edge of the desert to visit friends. With a warm welcome, the host led us to a terrace at the front of the house where we all sat talking over traditional Omani coffee and dates. Our host's camels were kept a little distance away. To our surprise, all the camels came to the wall surrounding the house and inquisitively stretched their necks to see who had come and what was going on.

A Dutch lady named Lilianne Donders, whom I knew personally, had travelled extensively by camel in the Rub Al Khali, the great Empty Quarter. I learned a lot about camels from Lilianne and was greatly interested in her desert adventures. One of the stories she had to tell was of a young camel who was extremely exhausted. After a short rest, the camel refused to stand up and resume the journey. Lilianne's companions tried their best to cajole the camel to stand up, but still he refused. So Lilianne went up to the camel and spoke quietly into his ear, saying, "*We know how very tired you are, but, as we are on the last leg of our journey, please stand up and walk.*" Would you believe it, the camel actually got up and started walking!

It is not only the camel that is a symbol of our age-old traditions. There is also an iconic traditional weapon - the *khanjar*, a curved dagger with an ornamental handle encased in a scabbard of beautifully wrought silver that today is worn at the waist with a belt on ceremonial occasions. We still dress in our customary Omani way with a distinctive gown and *mussar* or turban. Our ancient forts and castles watch over the land and sea just as they did in centuries past. Oman's towns and cities have maintained their character in low-rise Arabian architecture. In a world caught up in modernity and globalism, all of this, our enduring traditional heritage, is very attractive to visitors. And yet we enjoy every modern convenience.

And so, this country, my country, the Sultanate of Oman, has come a long way in a remarkably short period of time. It is a wonderful feeling to be part of the great surge of change that propelled us into the late twentieth and early twenty-first centuries – and has not lost momentum.

Oman, with its exceptional hospitality and spectacular scenery is no longer the world's best kept secret. The recent expansion of Oman's tourism sector in a highly competitive global market is testament to the drawing power of the Sultanate as a favoured destination. As Oman reasserts its character as a cosmopolitan civilization, it is very exciting for me - and satisfying too, because I feel very much at home in such a culture.

All this is not to say that everything is perfectly rosy - there are no Utopias on earth. I have not hesitated in these memoirs to express my view that there should be more open discussion of issues and problems with constructive criticism aimed at progressive improvement. This chapter was written before the unrest that started in March of 2011 and I am very pleased to be able to state as we go to press that steps have been taken to ensure a more open and fair society with greater employment opportunities.

What I will say as the note on which to end this penultimate chapter is that it is tremendously gratifying that our Sultan, His Majesty Sultan Qaboos bin Said, is known to the world as a man of peace and the environment. What more could we hope for in today's world?

All's well that ends well

I am once again on the shores of Zanzibar. Gentle breezes bring the peaceful sound of ocean waves, above which I hear the familiar, happy chatter of my grandchildren. The family has gathered for a holiday at my daughter Rawya's idyllic retreat on the beach near Zanzibar Town. The house is large and comfortable – perfect for our extended family. All around is the most beautiful scenery. It is truly paradise on earth.

When my grandfather set out from Barka on camelback more than a century ago and made the long voyage over the seas to Zanzibar, he could not have imagined the legacy he would leave for succeeding generations. Nor, indeed, when I was in prison five decades ago and my world had fallen apart, could I have pictured a future as full of blessings as this. And there is every reason to believe that my grandchildren will enjoy an old age as satisfying as mine, if they are ambitious and hardworking and follow their dreams.

At this stage in life, I often find myself lost in thought. I am not daydreaming, but thinking of the meaning of a life long-lived. This book is not simply the story of my life and times; it is a reflection on the meaning of one man's life and what of value can be distilled for the reader.

After almost a century on this earth in the best and worst of times, I have come to know that nothing is permanent except what we believe in. A wise Oriental sage once said the only disability in life is a bad attitude. To cope with life in any era, courage is needed. And optimism. But even more essential is the family.

My family, like my religion, is more than an emblem of identity and a bedrock of values - it is, and always has been, a source of strength, inspiration, confidence and support.

I have lived in challenging times, not only because of the Revolution in Zanzibar, but with the momentous change that ushered in the modern world. Child of an old feudal world, I will one day say goodbye to the marvels of the twenty-first century.

My grandchildren and their children are the continuation of my life. I cannot know the nature of the world that they will experience half a century or more from now, nor do I wish the human life span to be extended. Unto everything there is a season.

I put my pen down now with a heart full of thanks for the fruits and flowers of the many seasons that were mine, and for what is yet to come.

The Author and his family today

The Author at home, January 2012

Border Design from a Traditional Zanzibari Kanga